The Pocket
PETER KROPOTKIN

The Pocket
PETER KROPOTKIN

Edited by Nathaniel Kennon Perkins

Trident Press
Boulder, CO

Published by Trident Press
940 Pearl St.
Boulder, CO 80302

ISBN: 978-0-9992499-4-9

Contents

EDITOR'S INTRODUCTION

———

I've done all the hip American anarchist lifestyle things. I've eaten out of dumpsters, lived in collective houses with 15 other people, dropped banners, volunteered at animal rescues, made tall bikes, started a homestead farm, busked, panhandled, gas-jugged, flown signs, written zines, been vegan, shoplifted, helped to run DIY spaces, practiced polyamory, traveled around the country, played in bands, declined to vote, voted, done drugs, written graffiti, kicked smoke grenades back at cops, been pepper-sprayed, blah blah blah.

I've met a lot of really beautiful and inspiring people doing these things. They've all had their own motivations for embracing anarchism, all of which are legitimate and rousing. Maybe they started out by witnessing racial injustice, or wanting to fight for animal rights, or seeing the planet get destroyed, or feeling oppressed because of their queerness. Maybe they saw a good punk show when they were a kid. Maybe they just didn't want to work or pay rent anymore.

All of these problems that exist in the world, all of this ugliness and injustice, are symptoms that stem from a common disease—capitalism. It's easy to get mad and fired up about it, channel that rage into the romanticism of the ex-worker mentality, and start singing folk punk songs. Good. It fucking should be. But it's also easy to start feeling tired and dirty and burned out when you're crowded into a space with a bunch of other people who are stressed out and depressed because they too had to grow up under capitalism. When you get scabies, when your comrades get too drunk to go dumpster diving and there's no food, when there are dishes in the sink and someone in your community turns out to be a piece-of-shit abuser. It's easy to be exhausted and forget why you started living for the revolution in the first place.

You realize that you have a bad haircut and you look stupid in a black bandanna.

You forget what the fuck anarchism even is.

This is why this book exists. It's a reminder that the lifestyle we love and hate, all the things we do and the fights we get into, come from somewhere. There is an actual political and economic philosophy behind it all, and it matters.

Peter Kropotkin knew this philosophy mattered, even from a young age. Born in Moscow on December 9, 1842, he had about everything in the world that a person could ask for. He was the son of a prince. His mother was the daughter of a rich and famous Cossack general. Kropotkin's family owned huge tracts of land and controlled over a thousand serfs. Kropotkin saw the injustice of this class system and rebelled harder than any pissed off teenager probably has since.

He travelled, went to prison, escaped, went into exile. He critiqued capitalism and feudalism for the way they manufactured poverty for many while promoting privilege for a few. He critiqued Marxist state communism for the hierarchal power structures it created and the inequality it maintained. He promoted mutual aid and self-sufficiency. He called for a four-hour workday. He acknowledged humans' flaws and competitive urges. He advocated communism, but a decentralized version of it, one in which people voluntarily created associations made of worker-run enterprises and self-governed communities.

Collected in this cute, pocket-sized volume are eight of Kropotkin's essays. The book starts with his indispensable article on anarchism, originally written for the Eleventh Edition of the *Encyclopedia Britannica*, and moves forward to expound on his ideas, which include prison abolition, syndicalism, expropriation, etc. While some of what is contained here seems outdated, the economic, political, and social principles ring true. Kropotkin's writings should not be forgotten if anarchists are going to keep putting one foot in front of the other.

— Nathaniel Kennon Perkins
Boulder, CO

ANARCHISM

ANARCHISM (from the Gr. *an*, and *archos*, contrary to authority), the name given to a principle or theory of life and conduct under which society is conceived without government — harmony in such a society being obtained, not by submission to law, or by obedience to any authority, but by free agreements concluded between the various groups, territorial and professional, freely constituted for the sake of production and consumption, as also for the satisfaction of the infinite variety of needs and aspirations of a civilized being. In a society developed on these lines, the voluntary associations which already now begin to cover all the fields of human activity would take a still greater extension so as to substitute themselves for the state in all its functions. They would represent an interwoven network, composed of an infinite variety of groups and federations of all sizes and degrees, local, regional, national and international temporary or more or less permanent — for all possible purposes: production, consumption and exchange, communications, sanitary arrangements, education, mutual protection, defense of the territory, and so on; and, on the other side, for the satisfaction of an ever-increasing number of scientific, artistic, literary and sociable needs. Moreover, such a society would represent nothing immutable. On the contrary — as is seen in organic life at large — harmony would (it is contended) result from an ever-changing adjustment and readjustment of equilibrium between the multitudes of forces and influences, and this adjustment would be the easier to obtain as none of the forces would enjoy a special protection from the state.

If, it is contended, society were organized on these principles, man would not be limited in the free exercise of his powers in productive work by a capitalist monopoly, maintained by the state; nor would he be limited in the exercise of his will by a fear of punishment, or by obedience towards individuals or metaphysical entities, which both lead to depression of initiative and servility of mind. He would be guided in his actions by his own understanding, which necessarily would bear the impression of a free action and reaction between his own self and the ethical conceptions of his surroundings. Man would thus be enabled to obtain the full development of all his faculties, intellectual, artistic and moral, without being hampered by overwork for the monopolists, or by the servility and inertia of mind of the great number. He would thus be able to reach *full individualization*, which is not possible either under the present system of individualism, or under any system of state socialism in the so-called *Volkstaat* (popular state).

The anarchist writers consider, moreover, that their conception is not a utopia, constructed on the *a priori* method, after a few desiderata have been taken as postulates. It is derived, they maintain, from an *analysis of tendencies* that are at work already, even though state socialism may find a temporary favor with the reformers. The progress of modern technics, which wonderfully simplifies the production of all the necessaries of life; the growing spirit of independence, and the rapid spread of free initiative and free understanding in all branches of activity — including those which formerly were considered as the proper attribution of church and state — are steadily reinforcing the no-government tendency.

As to their economical conceptions, the anarchists, in common with all socialists, of whom they constitute the left wing, maintain that the now prevailing system of private ownership in land, and our capitalist production for the sake of profits, represent a monopoly which runs against both the principles of justice and the dictates of utility. They are the main obstacle which prevents the successes of modern technics from being brought into the service of all, so as to produce general well-being. The anarchists consider the wage-system and capitalist production altogether as an obstacle to progress. But they point out also that the state was, and continues to be, the chief instrument for permitting the few to monopolize the land, and the capitalists to appropriate for themselves a quite disproportionate share of the yearly accumulated surplus of production. Consequently, while combating the present monopolization of land, and capitalism altogether, the anarchists combat with the same energy the state, as the main support of that system. Not this or that special form, but the state altogether, whether it be a monarchy or even a republic governed by means of the *referendum*.

The state organization, having always been, both in ancient and modern history (Macedonian Empire, Roman Empire, modern European states grown up on the ruins of the autonomous cities), the instrument for establishing monopolies in favor of the ruling minorities, cannot be made to work for the destruction of these monopolies. The anarchists consider, therefore, that to hand over to the state all the main sources of economical life — the land, the mines, the railways, banking, insurance, and so on — as also the management of all the main branches of industry, in addition to all the functions already accumulated in its hands (education, state-supported religions, defense of the territory, etc.), would mean to create a new instrument of tyranny. State capitalism would only increase the powers of bureaucracy and capitalism. True progress lies in the direction of decentralization, both *territorial* and *functional*, in the development of the spirit of local and personal initiative, and of free federation from the simple to the compound, in lieu of the present hierarchy from the center to the periphery.

In common with most socialists, the anarchists recognize that, like all evolution in nature, the slow evolution of society is followed from time to time by periods of accelerated evolution which are called revolutions; and they think that the era of revolutions is not yet closed. Periods of rapid changes will follow the periods of slow evolution, and these periods must be taken advantage of — not for increasing and widening the powers of the state, but for reducing them, through the organization in every township or commune of the local groups of producers and consumers, as also the regional, and eventually the international, federations of these groups.

In virtue of the above principles the anarchists refuse to be party to the present state organization and to support it by infusing fresh blood into it. They do not seek to constitute, and invite the working men not to constitute, political parties in the parliaments. Accordingly, since the foundation of the International Working Men's Association in 1864–1866, they have endeavored to promote their ideas directly amongst the labor organizations and to induce those unions to a direct struggle against capital, without placing their faith in parliamentary legislation.

The historical development of anarchism

The conception of society just sketched, and the tendency which is its dynamic expression, have always existed in mankind, in opposition to the governing hierarchic conception and tendency — now the one and now the other taking the upper hand at different periods of history. To the former tendency we owe the evolution, by the masses themselves, of those institutions — the clan, the village community, the guild, the free medieval city — by means of which the masses resisted the encroachments of the conquerors and the power-seeking minorities. The same tendency asserted itself with great energy in the great religious movements of medieval times, especially in the early movements of the reform and its forerunners. At the same time it evidently found its expression in the writings of some thinkers, since the times of Lao-tsze, although, owing to its non-scholastic and popular origin, it obviously found less sympathy among the scholars than the opposed tendency.

As has been pointed out by Prof. Adler in his *Geschichte des Sozialismus und Kommunismus*, Aristippus (430 BC), one of the founders of the Cyrenaic school, already taught that the wise must not give up their liberty to the state, and in reply to a question by Socrates he said that he did not desire to belong either to the governing or the governed class. Such an attitude, however, seems to have been dictated merely by an Epicurean attitude towards the life of the masses.

The best exponent of anarchist philosophy in ancient Greece was Zeno (342–267 or 270 BC), from Crete, the founder of the Stoic philosophy, who distinctly opposed his conception of a free community without government to the state-utopia of Plato. He repudiated the omnipotence of the state, its intervention and regimentation, and proclaimed the sovereignty of the moral law of the individual — remarking already that, while the necessary instinct of self-preservation leads man to egotism, nature has supplied a corrective to it by providing man with another instinct — that of sociability. When men are reasonable enough to follow their natural instincts, they will unite across the frontiers and constitute the cosmos. They will have no need of law-courts or police, will have no temples and no public worship, and use no money — free gifts taking the place of the exchanges. Unfortunately, the writings of Zeno have not reached us and are only known through fragmentary quotations. However, the fact that his very wording is similar to the wording now in use, shows how deeply is laid the tendency of human nature of which he was the mouthpiece.

In medieval times we find the same views on the state expressed by the illustrious bishop of Alba, Marco Girolamo Vida, in his first dialogue *De dignitate reipublicae* (Ferd. Cavalli, in *Mem. dell'Istituto Veneto, xiii.*; Dr E. Nys, *Researches in the History of Economics*). But it is especially in several early Christian movements, beginning with the ninth century in Armenia, and in the preachings of the early Hussites, particularly Chojecki, and the early Anabaptists, especially Hans Denk (cf. Keller, *Ein Apostel der Wiedertaufer*), that one finds the same ideas forcibly expressed — special stress being laid of course on their moral aspects.

Rabelais and Fenelon, in their utopias, have also expressed similar ideas, and they were also current in the eighteenth century amongst the French Encyclopaedists, as may be concluded from separate expressions occasionally met with in the writings of Rousseau, from Diderot's Preface to the Voyage of Bougainville, and so on. However, in all probability such ideas could not be developed then, owing to the rigorous censorship of the Roman Catholic Church.

These ideas found their expression later during the great French Revolution. While the Jacobins did all in their power to centralize everything in the hands of the government, it appears now, from recently published documents, that the masses of the people, in their municipalities and 'sections', accomplished a considerable constructive work. They appropriated for themselves the election of the judges, the organization of supplies and equipment for the army, as also for the large cities, work for the unemployed, the management of charities, and so on. They even tried to establish a direct correspondence between the 36,000 communes of France through the intermediary of a special board, outside the National Assembly (cf. Sigismund Lacroix, *Actes de la commune de Paris*).

It was Godwin, in his *Enquiry concerning Political Justice* (2 vols., 1793), who was the first to formulate the political and economical conceptions of anarchism, even though he did not give that name to the ideas developed in his remarkable work. Laws, he wrote, are not a product of the wisdom of our ancestors: they are the product of their passions, their timidity, their jealousies and their ambition. The remedy they offer is worse than the evils they pretend to cure. If and only if all laws and courts were abolished, and the decisions in the arising contests were left to reasonable men chosen for that purpose, real justice would gradually be evolved. As to the state, Godwin frankly claimed its abolition. A society, he wrote, can perfectly well exist without any government: only the communities should be small and perfectly autonomous. Speaking of property, he stated that the rights of every one 'to every substance capable of contributing to the benefit of a human being' must be regulated by justice alone: the substance must go 'to him who most wants it'. His conclusion was communism. Godwin, however, had not the courage to maintain his opinions. He entirely rewrote later on his chapter on property and mitigated his communist views in the second edition of *Political Justice* (8vo, 1796).

Proudhon was the first to use, in 1840 (*Qu'est-ce que la propriete?* first memoir), the name of anarchy with application to the no government state of society. The name of 'anarchists' had been freely applied during the French Revolution by the Girondists to those revolutionaries who did not consider that the task of the Revolution was accomplished with the overthrow of Louis XVI, and insisted upon a series of economical measures being taken (the abolition of feudal rights without redemption, the return to the village communities of the communal lands enclosed since 1669, the limitation of landed property to 120 acres, progressive income-tax, the national organization of exchanges on a just value basis, which already received a beginning of practical realization, and so on).

Now Proudhon advocated a society without government, and used the word anarchy to describe it. Proudhon repudiated, as is known, all schemes of communism, according to which mankind would be driven into communistic monasteries or barracks, as also

all the schemes of state or state-aided socialism which were advocated by Louis Blanc
and the collectivists. When he proclaimed
in his first memoir on property that 'Property is theft', he meant only property in its
present, Roman-law, sense of 'right of use
and abuse'; in property-rights, on the other
hand, understood in the *limited sense of possession*, he saw the best protection against the
encroachments of the state. At the same
time he did not want violently to dispossess
the present owners of land, dwelling-hous-
es, mines, factories and so on. He preferred
to attain the same end by rendering capital
incapable of earning interest; and this he
proposed to obtain by means of a national
bank, based on the mutual confidence of all
those who are engaged in production, who
would agree to exchange among themselves
their produces at cost-value, by means of labor checks representing the hours of labor
required to produce every given commodity.
Under such a system, which Proudhon described as 'Mutuellisme', all the exchanges of
services would be strictly equivalent. Besides,
such a bank would be enabled to lend money
without interest, levying only something like
one percent, or even less, for covering the

cost of administration. Everyone being thus enabled to borrow the money that would be required to buy a house, nobody would agree to pay any more a yearly rent for the use of it. A general 'social liquidation' would thus be rendered easy, without violent expropriation. The same applied to mines, railways, factories and so on.

In a society of this type the state would be useless. The chief relations between citizens would be based on free agreement and regulated by mere account keeping. The contests might be settled by arbitration. A penetrating criticism of the state and all possible forms of government, and a deep insight into all economic problems, were well-known characteristics of Proudhon's work.

It is worth noticing that French mutualism had its precursor in England, in William Thompson, who began by mutualism before he became a communist, and in his followers John Gray (*A Lecture on Human Happiness*, 1825; *The Social System,* 1831) and J. F. Bray (*Labour's Wrongs and Labour's Remedy*, 1839). It had also its precursor in America. Josiah Warren, who was born in 1798 (cf. W. Bailie, *Josiah Warren, the First American Anarchist*, Boston, 1900), and belonged to Owen's 'New

Harmony', considered that the failure of this enterprise was chiefly due to the suppression of individuality and the lack of initiative and responsibility. These defects, he taught, were inherent to every scheme based upon authority and the community of goods. He advocated, therefore, complete individual liberty. In 1827 he opened in Cincinnati a little country store which was the first 'equity store', and which the people called 'time store', because it was based on labor being exchanged hour for hour in all sorts of produce. 'Cost — the limit of price', and consequently 'no interest', was the motto of his store, and later on of his 'equity village', near New York, which was still in existence in 1865. Mr. Keith's 'House of Equity' at Boston, founded in 1855, is also worthy of notice.

While the economical, and especially the mutual-banking, ideas of Proudhon found supporters and even a practical application in the United States, his political conception of anarchy found but little echo in France, where the Christian socialism of Lamennais and the Fourierists, and the state socialism of Louis Blanc and the followers of Saint-Simon, were dominating. These ideas found, however, some temporary support among the left-wing Hegelians in Germany, Moses Hess in 1843, and Karl Grün in 1845, who advocated anarchism. Besides, the authoritarian communism of Wilhelm Weitling having given origin to opposition amongst the Swiss working men, Wilhelm Marr gave expression to it in the forties.

On the other side, individualist anarchism found, also in Germany, its fullest expression in Max Stirner (Kaspar Schmidt), whose remarkable works (*Der Einzige und sein Eigenthum* and articles contributed to the *Rheinische Zeitung*) remained quite overlooked until they were brought into prominence by John Henry Mackay.

Prof. V. Basch, in a very able introduction to his interesting book, *L'Individualisme anarchiste*: *Max Stirner* (1904), has shown how the development of the German philosophy from Kant to Hegel, and 'the absolute' of Schelling and the Geist of Hegel, necessarily provoked, when the anti-Hegelian revolt began, the preaching of the same 'absolute' in the camp of the rebels. This was done by Stirner, who advocated, not only a complete revolt against the state and against the servitude which authoritarian communism would impose upon men, but also the full liberation of the individual from all social and moral bonds — the rehabilitation of the 'I', the supremacy of the individual, complete 'amoralism', and the 'association of the egotists'. The final conclusion of that sort of individual anarchism has been indicated by Prof. Basch. It maintains that the aim of all superior civilization is, not to permit all members of the community to develop in a normal way, but to permit certain better-endowed individuals 'fully to develop', even at the cost of the happiness and the very existence of the mass of mankind. It is thus a return towards the most common individualism, advocated by all the would-be superior minorities, to which indeed man owes in his history precisely the state and the rest, which these individualists combat. Their individualism goes so far as to end in a negation of their own starting-point — to say nothing of the impossibility for the individual to attain a really full development in the conditions of oppression of the masses by the 'beautiful aristocracies'. His development would remain unilateral. This is why this direction of thought, notwithstanding its undoubtedly correct and useful advocacy of the full development of each individuality, finds a hearing only in limited artistic and literary circles.

Anarchism in the International Working Men's Association

A general depression in the propaganda of all fractions of socialism followed, as is known, after the defeat of the uprising of the Paris working men in June 1848 and the fall of the Republic. All the socialist press was gagged during the reaction period, which lasted fully twenty years. Nevertheless, even anarchist thought began to make some progress, namely in the writings of Bellegarrique (Caeurderoy), and especially Joseph Déjacque (*Les Lazareacute'ennes, L 'Humanisphère*, an anarchist-communist utopia, lately discovered and reprinted). The socialist movement revived only after 1864, when some French working men, all 'mutualists', meeting in London during the Universal Exhibition with English followers of Robert Owen, founded the International Working Men's Association. This association developed very rapidly and adopted a policy of direct economical struggle against capitalism, without interfering in the political parliamentary agitation, and this policy was followed until 1871. However, after the Franco-German War, when the International Association was prohibited in France after the uprising of the Commune, the German working men, who had received manhood suffrage for elections to the newly constituted imperial parliament, insisted upon modifying the tactics of the International, and began to build up a Social Democratic political party. This soon led to a division in the Working Men's Association, and the Latin federations, Spanish, Italian, Belgian and Jurassic (France could not be represented), constituted among themselves a Federal union which broke entirely with the Marxist general council of the International. Within these federations developed now what may be described as *modern anarchism*. After the names of 'Federalists' and 'Anti-authoritarians' had been used for some time by these federations the name of 'anarchists', which their adversaries insisted upon applying to them, prevailed, and finally it was revindicated.

Bakunin soon became the leading spirit among these Latin federations for the development of the principles of anarchism, which he did in a number of writings, pamphlets and letters. He demanded the complete abolition of the state, which — he wrote — is a product of religion, belongs to a lower state of civilization, represents the negation of liberty, and spoils even that which it undertakes to do for the sake of general wellbeing. The state was a historically necessary evil, but its complete extinction will be, sooner or later, equally necessary. Repudiating all legislation, even when issuing from universal suffrage, Bakunin claimed for each nation, each region and each commune, full autonomy, so long as it is not a menace to its neighbors, and full independence for the individual, adding that one becomes really free only when, and in proportion as, all others are free. Free federations of the communes would constitute free nations.

As to his economical conceptions, Bakunin described himself, in common with his Federalist comrades of the International (César De Paepe, James Guillaume, Schwitzguébel), a 'collectivist anarchist' — not in the sense of Vidal and Pecqueur in the 1840s, or of their modern Social Democratic followers, but to express a state of things in which all necessaries for production are owned in common by the labor groups and the free communes, while the ways of retribution of labor, communist or otherwise, would be settled by each group for itself. Social revolution, the near approach of which was foretold at that time by all socialists, would be the means of bringing into life the new conditions.

The Jurassic, the Spanish and the Italian federations and sections of the International Working Men's Association, as also the French, the German and the American anarchist groups, were for the next years the chief centers of anarchist thought and propaganda. They refrained from any participation in parliamentary politics, and always kept in close contact with the labor organizations. However, in the second half of the 'eighties and the early 'nineties of the nineteenth century, when the influence of the anarchists began to be felt in strikes, in the First of May demonstrations, where they promoted the idea of a general strike for an eight hours' day, and in the anti-militarist propaganda in the army, violent prosecutions were directed against them, especially in the Latin countries (including physical torture in the Barcelona Castle) and the United States (the execution of five Chicago anarchists in 1887). Against these prosecutions the anarchists retaliated by acts of violence which in their turn were followed by more executions from above, and new acts of revenge from below. This created in the general public the impression that violence is the substance of anarchism, a view repudiated by its supporters, who hold that in reality violence is resorted to by all parties in proportion as their open action is obstructed by repression, and exceptional laws render them outlaws. (Cf. *Anarchism and Outrage*, by C. M. Wilson, and *Report of the Spanish Atrocities Committee*, in 'Freedom Pamphlets'; *A Concise History of the Great Trial of the Chicago Anarchists*, by Dyer Lum (New York, 1886); *The Chicago Martyrs: Speeches*, etc.).

Anarchism continued to develop, partly in the direction of Proudhonian 'mutuellisme', but chiefly as communist-anarchism, to which a third direction, Christian-anarchism, was added by Leo Tolstoy, and a fourth, which might be ascribed as literary-anarchism, began amongst some prominent modern writers.

The ideas of Proudhon, especially as regards mutual banking, corresponding with those of Josiah Warren, found a considerable following in the United States, creating quite a school, of which the main writers are Stephen Pearl Andrews, William Grene, Lysander Spooner (who began to write in 1850, and whose unfinished work, *Natural Law*, was full of promise), and several others, whose names will be found in Dr Nettlau's *Bibliographie de l'anarchie*.

A prominent position among the individualist anarchists in America has been occupied by Benjamin R. Tucker, whose journal Liberty was started in 1881 and whose conceptions are a combination of those of Proudhon with those of Herbert Spencer. Starting from the statement that anarchists are egotists, strictly speaking, and that every group of individuals, be it a secret league of a few persons, or the Congress of the United States, has the right to oppress all mankind, provided it has the power to do so, that equal liberty for all and absolute equality ought to be the law, and 'mind every one your own business' is the unique moral law of anarchism, Tucker goes on to prove that a general and thorough application of these principles would be beneficial and would offer no danger, because the powers of every individual would be limited by the exercise of the equal rights of all others. He further indicated (following H. Spencer) the difference which exists between the encroachment on

somebody's rights and resistance to such an
encroachment; between domination and
defense: the former being equally condem-
nable, whether it be encroachment of a crim-
inal upon an individual, or the encroachment
of one upon all others, or of all others upon
one; while resistance to encroachment is de-
fensible and necessary. For their self-defense,
both the citizen and the group have the right
to any violence, including capital punishment. Violence is also justified for enforcing
the duty of keeping an agreement. Tucker
thus follows Spencer, and, like him, opens
(in the present writer's opinion) the way for
reconstituting under the heading of 'defense'
all the functions of the state. His criticism
of the present state is very searching, and his
defense of the rights of the individual very
powerful. As regards his economical views B.
R. Tucker follows Proudhon.

The individualist anarchism of the
American Proudhonians finds, however, but
little sympathy amongst the working masses. Those who profess it — they are chiefly
'intellectuals' — soon realize that the *individualization* they so highly praise is not
attainable by individual efforts, and either
abandon the ranks of the anarchists, and are

driven into the liberal individualism of the classical economist or they retire into a sort of Epicurean amoralism, or superman theory, similar to that of Stirner and Nietzsche. The great bulk of the anarchist working men prefer the anarchist-communist ideas which have gradually evolved out of the anarchist collectivism of the International Working Men's Association. To this direction belong — to name only the better known exponents of anarchism Elisée Reclus, Jean Grave, Sebastien Faure, Emile Pouget in France; Errico Malatesta and Covelli in Italy; R. Mella, A. Lorenzo, and the mostly unknown authors of many excellent manifestos in Spain; John Most amongst the Germans; Spies, Parsons and their followers in the United States, and so on; while Domela Nieuwenhuis occupies an intermediate position in Holland. The chief anarchist papers which have been published since 1880 also belong to that direction; while a number of anarchists of this direction have joined the so-called syndicalist movement- the French name for the non-political labor movement, devoted to direct struggle with capitalism, which has lately become so prominent in Europe.

As one of the anarchist-communist direction, the present writer for many years endeavored to develop the following ideas: to show the intimate, logical connection which exists between the modern philosophy of natural sciences and anarchism; to put anarchism on a scientific basis by the study of the tendencies that are apparent now in society and may indicate its further evolution; and to work out the basis of anarchist ethics. As regards the substance of anarchism itself, it was Kropotkin's aim to prove that communism at least partial — has more chances of being established than collectivism, especially in communes taking the lead, and that free, or anarchist-communism is the only form of communism that has any chance of being accepted in civilized societies; communism and anarchy are therefore two terms of evolution which complete each other, the one rendering the other possible and acceptable. He has tried, moreover, to indicate how, during a revolutionary period, a large city — if its inhabitants have accepted the idea could organize itself on the lines of free communism; the city guaranteeing to every inhabitant dwelling, food and clothing to an extent corresponding to the comfort now available to the middle classes only, in exchange for a half-day's, or five-hours' work; and how all those things which would be considered as luxuries might be obtained by everyone if he joins for the other half of the day all sorts of free associations pursuing all possible aims — educational, literary, scientific, artistic, sports and so on. In order to prove the first of these assertions he has analyzed the possibilities of agriculture and industrial work, both being combined with brain work. And in order to elucidate the main factors of human evolution, he has analyzed the part played in history by the popular constructive agencies of mutual aid and the historical role of the state.

Without naming himself an anarchist, Leo Tolstoy, like his predecessors in the popular religious movements of the fifteenth and sixteenth centuries, Chojecki, Denk and many others, took the anarchist position as regards the state and property rights, deducing his conclusions from the general spirit of the teachings of the Christ and from the necessary dictates of reason. With all the might of his talent he made (especially in *The Kingdom of God in Yourselves*) a powerful criticism of the church, the state and law altogether, and especially of the present property laws.

He describes the state as the domination of the wicked ones, supported by brutal force. Robbers, he says, are far less dangerous than a well-organized government. He makes a searching criticism of the prejudices which are current now concerning the benefits conferred upon men by the church, the state and the existing distribution of property, and from the teachings of the Christ he deduces the rule of non-resistance and the absolute condemnation of all wars. His religious arguments are, however, so well combined with arguments borrowed from a dispassionate observation of the present evils, that the anarchist portions of his works appeal to the religious and the non-religious reader alike.

It would be impossible to represent here, in a short sketch, the penetration, on the one hand, of anarchist ideas into modern literature, and the influence, on the other hand, which the libertarian ideas of the best contemporary writers have exercised upon the development of anarchism. One ought to consult the ten big volumes of the *Supplément Littéraire* to the paper *La Révolte* and later the *Temps Nouveaux*, which contain reproductions from the works of hundreds of modern authors expressing anarchist ideas, in order to realize how closely anarchism is connected with all the intellectual movement of our own times. J. S. Mill's *Liberty*, Spencer's *Individual versus the State*, Marc Guyau's *Morality without Obligation or Sanction*, and Fouillée's *La Morale, l'art et la religion*, the works of Multatuli (E. Douwes Dekker), Richard Wagner's *Art and Revolution*, the works of Nietzsche, Emerson, W. Lloyd Garrison, Thoreau, Alexander Herzen, Edward Carpenter and so on; and in the domain of fiction, the dramas of Ibsen, the poetry of Walt Whitman, Tolstoy's *War and Peace*, Zola's *Paris* and *Le Travail*, the latest works of Merezhkovsky, and an infinity of works of less known authors, are full of ideas which show how closely anarchism is interwoven with the work that is going on in modern thought in the same direction of enfranchisement of man from the bonds of the state as well as from those of capitalism.

EXPROPRIATION

I.

It is told of Rothschild that, seeing his fortune threatened by the revolution of 1849, he hit upon the following stratagem: — "I am quite willing to admit," said he, "that my fortune has been accumulated at the expense of others, but if it were divided among the millions of Europe tomorrow the share of each would only amount to five schillings if he asks me for it."

Having given due publicity to his promise, our millionaire proceeded as usual to stroll quietly through the streets of Frankfort. Three or four passersby asked for their five schillings, which he disbursed with a sardonic smile. His stratagem succeeded and the family of the millionaire is still in possession of its wealth.

Expropriation

It is in much the same fashion that the shrewd heads among the middle classes reason when they say, "Ah, expropriation, I know what that means. You take all of the topcoats and lay them in a heap, and everyone is free to help himself and fight for the best."

But such jests are irrelevant as well as flippant. What we want is not a redistribution of topcoats. Besides, it is likely that in such a general scramble the shivering folk would come off any better? Nor do we want to divide up the wealth of the Rothchilds. What we do want is so to arrange things that every human being born into the world shall be ensured the opportunity in the first instance of learning some useful occupation, and of becoming skilled in it; next, that he shall be free to work at his trade without asking leave of master or owner, and without handing over to landlord or capitalists the lion's share of what he produces. As to the wealth held by the Rothchilds or the Vanderbilts, it will serve us to organize our system of communal production.

The day when the laborer may till the ground without paying away half of what he produces, the day when the machines necessary to prepare the soil for rich harvests are at the free disposal of the cultivators, the day when the worker in the factory produces for the community and not for the monopolist — that day will see the workers clothed and fed; and there will be no more Rothchilds or other exploiters. No one will then have to sell his working power for a wage that only represents a fraction of what he produces.

"So far good," say our critics, "but you will have Rothchilds coming in from outside. How are you to prevent a person from amassing millions in China and then settling amongst you? How are you going to prevent such a one from surrounding himself with lackeys and wage slaves — from exploiting them and enriching himself at their expense?"

"You cannot bring about a revolution all over the world at the same time. Well then. Are you going to establish Custom Houses on your frontiers, to search all who enter your country, and confiscate the money they bring with them? — Anarchist policemen firing on travelers would be a fine spectacle!"

But at the root of this argument there is a great error. Those who propound it have never paused to inquire whence come the fortunes of the rich. A little thought would suffice to show them that these fortunes have their beginning in the poverty of the poor. When there are no longer any destitute there will no longer be any rich to exploit them.

Let us glance for a moment at the middle ages, when great fortunes began to spring up.

A feudal baron seizes on a fertile valley. But as long as the fertile valley is empty of folk our baron is not rich. His land brings him in nothing, he might as well possess a property in the moon. Now what does our baron do to enrich himself? He looks out for peasants!

But if every peasant-farmer had a piece of land, free from rent and taxes, if he had in addition the tools and stock necessary for farm labor, who would plough the lands of the baron? Each would look after his own. But there are whole tribes of destitute persons ruined by wars, or drought, or pestilence. They have neither horse nor plough (Iron was costly in the middle ages, and a draught-horse still more so).

All these destitute creatures are trying to better their condition. One day they see on the road at the confines of our baron's estate a notice-board indicating by certain signs adapted to their comprehension that the laborer who is willing to settle on this estate will receive the tools and materials to build his cottage and sow his fields, and a portion of land rent free for a certain number of years. The number of years is represented by so many crosses on the signboard, and the peasant understands the meaning of these crosses.

So the poor wretches swarm over the baron's lands, making roads, draining marshes, building villages. In nine years he begins to tax them. Five years later he levies rent. Then he doubles it. The peasant accepts these new conditions because he cannot find better ones elsewhere; and little by little, by the aid of laws made by the oppressors, the poverty of the peasants becomes the source of the landlord's wealth. And it is not only the Lord of the Manor who preys upon him. A whole host of usurers swoop down upon the villages, increasing as the wretchedness of the peasants increases. That is how thing went in the Middle Ages; and today is still not the same thing? If there were free lands which the peasant could cultivate if he pleased, would he pay 50 to some "Shabble of a Duke" for condescending to sell him a scrap? Would he burden himself with a lease which absorbed a third of the produce? Would he — on the metayer system — consent to give the half of his harvest to the landowner?

But he has nothing. So he will accept any conditions, if only he can keep body and soul together, while he tills the soil and enriches the landlord.

So in the nineteenth century, just as in the Middle Ages, the poverty of the peasant is a source of wealth to the landed proprietor.

II.

The landlord owes his riches to the poverty of the peasants, and the wealth of the capitalists comes from the same source.

Take the case of a citizen of the middle class who, somehow or other, finds himself in possession of 20,000. He could, of course, spend his money at rate of 2,000 a year, a mere bagatelle in these days of fantastic, senseless luxury. But then he would have nothing left at the end of ten years. So, being a "practical person," he prefers to keep his fortune intact, and win for himself a snug little annual income as well.

That is very easy in our society, for the good reason that the towns and villages swarm with workers who have not the wherewithal to live for a month, or even a fortnight. So our worthy citizen starts a factory: the banks hasten to lend him another 20,000, especially if he has a reputation for "business ability"; and with this round sum he can command the labor of five hundred hands.

If all the men and women in the country-side had their daily bread sure and their daily needs already satisfied, who would work for our capitalists, or be willing to manufacture for him, at a wage of half-a-crown a day, commodities selling in the market for a crown or even more?

Unhappily — we know it all too well — the poor quarters of our towns and the neighboring villages are full of needy wretches, whose children clamor for bread. So, before the factory is well finished, the workers hasten to offer themselves. Where a hundred required a thousand besiege the doors, and from the time his mill started the owner, if he is not more than commonly stupid, will clear 40 a year out of each mill hand he employs.

He is thus able to lay by a snug little fortune, and if he chooses a lucrative trade, and if he has "business talents," he will increase his income by doubling the number of the men he exploits.

So he becomes a personage of importance. He can afford to give dinners to other personages, to the local magnates, the civic, legal, and political dignitaries. With his money he can "marry money," by-and-by he may pick and choose places for his children, and later on perhaps get something good from the government — a contract for the army or for the police. His gold breeds gold; till at last a war, or even a rumor of war, or a speculation on the Stock Exchange, gives him his great opportunity.

Nine-tenths of the huge fortunes made in the United States are (as Henry George has shown in his "Social Problems") the result of knavery on a large scale, assisted by the state. In Europe nine-tenths of the fortunes made in our monarchies and republics have the same origin. There are not two ways of becoming a millionaire.

This is the secret of wealth; find the starving and destitute, pay them half a crown, and make them produce ten schillings worth in the day, amass a fortune by the means, and then increase it by some lucky hit, made with help of the State.

Need we go on to speak of small fortunes attributed by the economists to forethought and frugality, when we know that mere saving in itself brings in nothing, so long as the pence saved are not used to exploit the famishing?

Take a shoemaker, for instance. Grant that his work is well paid, that he has plenty of custom, and that by dint of strict frugality he contrives to lay by from eighteen pence to two schillings a day, perhaps a month.

Grant that our shoemaker is never ill, that he does not half starve himself, in spite of his passion for economy; that he does not marry or that he has no children; that he does not die of consumption; suppose anything and everything you please!

Well, at the age of fifty he will not have scraped together 800; and he will not have enough to live on during his old age, when he is past work. Assuredly this is not how great fortunes are made. But suppose our shoemaker, as soon as he laid by a few pence, thriftily conveys them to the savings-bank, and that the savings bank lends them to capitalists who is just about to "employ labor" — i.e., to exploit the poor. Then our shoemaker takes an apprentice, the child of some poor wretch who will think himself lucky if in five years time his son has learned the trade and is able to earn a living.

Expropriation

Meanwhile our shoemaker does not lose by him; and if trade is brisk he soon takes a second, and then a third apprentice. By-and-by he will take two or three journeymen—poor wretches, thankful to receive a half-a-crown a day for work that is worth five shillings, and if our shoemaker is "in luck," that is to say, if he is keen enough and mean enough, his journeymen and apprentices will bring him in nearly one a day, over and above the product of his own toil. He can then enlarge his business. He will gradually become rich, and no longer have any need to stint himself in the necessaries of life. He will leave a snug little fortune to his son.

That is what people call "being economical and having frugal, temperate habits." At bottom it is nothing more nor less than grinding the face of the poor.

Commerce seems an exception to this rule. "Such a man," we are told, "buys tea in China, brings it to France and realizes a profit of thirty percent. On his original outlay, he has exploited nobody.

Nevertheless, the case is analogous. If our merchant had carried his bales on his back, well and good! In early medieval times, that was exactly how foreign trade was conducted, and so no one reached such giddy heights of fortune as in our days. Very few, and very hardly earned, were the gold coins which the medieval merchant gained from a long and dangerous voyage. It was less the love of money than the thirst of travel and adventure that inspired his undertakings.

Nowadays the method is simpler. A merchant who has some capital need not stir from his desk to become wealthy. He telegraphs to an agent telling him to buy a hundred tons of tea, he freights a ship, the vessel brings him his cargo. He does not even take the risks of the voyage, for his tea and his vessel are insured, and if he has expended four thousand pounds he will receive more than five thousand: that is to say, if he has not attempted to speculate in some novel commodities, in which case he runs a chance of either doubling his fortune or losing it altogether.

Now, how could he find men willing to cross the sea, to travel to China and back, to endure hardship and slavish toil and to risk their lives for a miserable pittance? How could he find dock laborers willing to load and unload his ships for "starvation wages?" How? Because they are needy and starving. Go to the sea — ports, visit — the cook shops and taverns on the quays, and look at these men who have come to hire themselves crowding round the dock gates, which they besiege from early dawn, hoping to be allowed to work on the vessels. Look at these sailors, happy to be hired for a long voyage, after weeks and months of waiting. All their lives long they have gone down to the sea in ships, and they sail in others still, until the day when they perish in the waves.

Enter the cabins, look at their wives and children in rags, living one knows not how till the fathers return, and you will have the answer to that question. Multiply examples; choose them where you will consider the origin of all fortunes, large or small, whether rising out of commerce, finance, manufacturers, or the land. Everywhere you will find that the health of the wealthy springs from the poverty of the poor. An Anarchist society need not fear the advent of an unknown Rothschild who would seek to settle in its midst If every member of the community knows that after a few hours of productive toil he will have a right to all the pleasures that civilization procures, and to those deeper sources of enjoyment which art and science offer to all who seek them, he will not sell his strength for a starvation wage. No one will volunteer to work for the enrichment of your Rothschild. His golden guineas will be only so many pieces of metal — useful for various purposes, but incapable of breeding more.

In answering the above objection we have at the sometime indicated the scope of Expropriation. It must extend to all that permits any one, no matter whom financer, mill-owner, or landlord, to appropriate the product of others' toil. Our formula is simple and comprehensive.

We do not want to rob any one of his coat, but we wish to give to the workers all those things that lack of which makes them fall an easy prey to the exploiter, and we will do our utmost that none shall lack aught, that not a single man shall be forced to sell the strength of his right arm to obtain a bare subsistence for himself and his babes. That is what we mean when we talk of expropriation; that will be our duty during the revolution, for whose coming we look, not two hundred years hence, but soon, very soon.

III.

The ideas of Anarchism in general and of Expropriation in particular find much more sympathy than when we apt to imagine among men of independent character, and those for whom idleness is not the supreme ideal. "Still," our friends often warn us, "take care you do not go too far! Humanity cannot be changed in a day, so do not be too great a hurry with your schemes of Expropriation on too small a scale to be lasting. We found not have the revolutionary impulse arrested in mid-career, to exhaust itself in half measures, which would content no-one, and which while producing a tremendous upheaval of society, and stopping its customary activities, would have no power of life in themselves, and would merely spread general discontent and inevitably prepare the way for triumph of reaction.

There are, in fact, in a modern state, established relations, which are practically impossible to modify if one attacks them only in detail. There are wheels within wheels in our economic organization — the machinery is so complex and interdependent that no one part can be modified without disturbing the whole. This will become clear as soon as an attempt is made to expropriate anything.

Let us suppose that in a certain country a limited form of Expropriation is effected; for example, that, as recently suggested by Henry George, only the property of the great landlords is confiscated, whilst the factories are left untouched; or that, in a certain city, house property is taken over by the commune, but merchandise is left in private ownership; or that, in some manufacturing center, the factories are communalized, but the land is not interfered with.

The same result would follow in each case — a terrible shattering of the industrial system, without the means of reorganizing it on new lines. Industry and commerce would be at a deadlock, yet a return to the first principles of justice would not have been achieved, and society would find itself powerless to construct a harmonious whole.

If agriculture could free itself from great landowners, while industry still remained the bond slave of the capitalists, the merchant, and the banker, nothing would be accomplished. The farmer suffers today not only in having to pay rent to the landlord; he is oppressed on all hands by existing conditions. He is exploited by the tradesman, who makes him pay half-a-crown for a spade which, measured by labor spent on it, is not worth more than sixpence. He is taxed by the state, which cannot do without its formidable hierarchy of officials, and finds it necessary to maintain an expensive army, because the traders of all nations are perpetually fighting for markets, and any day a little quarrel arising from the exploitation of some part of Asia or Africa may result in war.

Then again, farmer and laborer suffer from the depopulation of country places: the young people are attracted to the large factory towns by the bait of high wages paid temporarily by the manufactures of articles of luxury, or by the attractions of a more stirring life. The artificial protection of industry, the industrial exploitation of foreign countries, the prevalence of stock-jobbing, the difficulty of improving the soil and the machinery of production — all these are causes which work together against agriculture, which indeed is burdened not only by rent, but by the whole complexity of conditions developed in a society based on exploitation. Thus, even if the expropriation of land were accomplished, and without paying rent, agriculture, even though it should enjoy — which can by no means be taken for granted — a momentary prosperity, would soon fall back into the slough in which it finds itself today.

The whole thing would have to begun over and over again, with increased difficulties.

The same holds true of industry. Take the converse case; make over the factories to those who work in them, but leave the agricultural laborers slaves to farmer and landlord. Abolish the master-manufacturers, but leave the land owner his land, the banker his money, the merchant his Exchange, maintain still the warm idlers who live on the toil of the workmen, the thousand and one middlemen, the State with its numberless officials, and industry would come to a stand-still. Finding no purchasers in the mass of country people still as poor as ever, having no raw material, unable to export products, and embarrassed by the stoppage of trade, industry could only struggle on feebly, and thousands of workers would be thrown upon the streets. These starving crowds would be ready and willing to submit to the first schemer who came to exploit them, they would even consent to return to the old slavery, if only under promise would work.

Or, finally, suppose you oust the land-owners and hand over the mills and factories to the worker without interfering with the swarm of middlemen who drain off the produce of our manufacturers and speculate in corn and flour, meat and groceries in our great centers of commerce. Well, when exchange is arrested and products cease to circulate, when London is without bread and Yorkshire finds no buyers for her cloth, a terrible counter-revolution trampling upon heaps of slain, sweeping the towns and villages with shot and shell; there will be proscriptions, panic, flight, perhaps all the towers of wholesale judicial massacre of the Guillotine, as in France in 1815, 1848, and 1871.

All is interdependent in a civilized society; it is impossible to reform any one thing without altering the whole. On that day when we strike at private property, under any one of its forms, territorial or industrial, we shall be obliged to attack all its manifestations. The very success of the Revolution will demand it.

Besides we could not if we would confine ourselves to a partial expropriation. Once the principle of the "Divine Right of Property" is shaken, no amount of theorizing will prevent its overthrow, here by the slaves of the soil, there by the slaves of the machine.

If a great town, Paris for example, were to confine itself to taken possession of the houses or the factories, it would still be forced to deny the right of the bankers to levy upon the Commune a tax amounting to 2,000,000, in the form of interest for former loans. The great city would be obliged to put itself in touch with the rural districts, and its influence would inevitably urge the peasants to free themselves from the landowner. It would be necessary to communalize the railways that the citizens might get food and work, and lastly, to prevent the waste of supplies, and to guard against the chicanery of corn-speculators, like those to whom the commune of 1793 fell a prey; it would place in the hands of the citizens the work of stocking their warehouses with their commodities, and apportioning the produce.

Nevertheless, some Socialists still seek to establish a distinction. "Of course," they say, "the soil, the mines, the mills and manufacturers must be expropriated; these are the instruments of production, and it is right we should consider them public property. But articles of consumption, food, clothes and dwellings, should remain private property."

Popular common sense has got the better of this subtle distinction. We are not savages who can live in the woods, without other shelter than the branches. The civilized man needs a roof and a hearth, a bed-chamber and a bed. It is true that the bed, the room and the house of the non-producer are only part of the paraphernalia of idleness. But for the worker a room, properly heated and lighted, is as much an instrument of production as the tool or the machine. It is the place where the nerves and sinews gather strength for the work of the morrow. The rest of the work-man is the daily repairing of the machine.

The same argument applies even more obviously to food. The so-called economists of whom we speak would hardly deny that the coal burnt in a machine could do no work, be excluded from the list of things indispens-able to the producer? Such hair-splitting is worthy of the metaphysic of the schoolmen. The rich man's feast is indeed a matter of luxury, but the food of the worker is just as much a part of production as the fuel burnt by the steam engine.

The same with clothing: if the econo-mists who draw this distinction between articles of production and of consumption dressed themselves in fashion of New Guin-ea we could understand their objection. But men who could not write a word without a shirt on their back are not in a position to draw such a hard and fast line between their shirt and their pen. And though the Dainty gowns of their dames must certainly rank as objects of luxury, there is nevertheless a certain quantity of linen, cotton and woolen stuff, which is a necessity of life to the producer. The shirt and shoes in which he goes off to work, his cap and the jacket he slips on after the day's toil is over, these are as necessary to him as the hammer to the anvil.

Whether we like it or not, that is what the people mean by a revolution. As soon as they have made a clean sweep of the Government, they will seek first of all to ensure to themselves descent dwellings and sufficient food and clothes — free of rent and taxes.

And the people will be right. The methods of the people will be much more in accordance with science than those of the economists who draw so many distinctions between instruments of production and articles of consumption. The people understand that this is just the point where the Revolution ought to begin; and they will lay the foundations of the only economic science worthy the name — a science which might be

Expropriation

called: "The Study of the Needs of Humanity, and of the Economic Means to satisfy them."

SYNDICALISM
& ANARCHISM

———————

From all sides, people are always asking us, "What is Syndicalism and what is its relationship to Anarchism?" Here we will do our best to answer these questions.

Syndicalism is only a new name for an old tactic in which the workers of Great Britain have taken successful refuge for a long time: the tactic of Direct Action, and the fight against Capital in the economic sphere. This tactic, in fact, was their favorite weapon. Not possessing the right to vote, British workers in the first half of the nineteenth century won important economic gains and created a strong trade union organization through use of this weapon alone and even forced the ruling classes to acknowledge their demands with legislation (including an extension of the franchise).

Syndicalism & Anarchism

Direct Action has proved itself, both in achieving economic results and in extracting political concessions, to be a significant weapon in the economic arena.

In Britain, the influence of this idea was so strong that in the years 1830 to 1831 Robert Owen attempted to found one big national union, and an international workers organization, which using direct action would struggle against Capital. Early fears of persecution by the British government forced him to abandon this idea.

This was followed by the Chartist movement, which used the powerful, widespread and partly secret worker's organizations of the time in order to gain considerable political concessions. At this point, British workers received their first lesson in politics: very soon they realized that although they backed political agitation with all means at their disposal, this agitation won them no economic advantages other than those they themselves forced the employers and lawgivers to concede through strikes and revolts. They realized how pointless it was to expect serious improvements to their conditions of life to come from parliament.

French workers came to exactly the same

conclusion: the revolution of 1848, which had given France a Republic, convinced them of the complete fruitlessness of political agitation and even of political victories; the only fundamental changes to workers conditions of life are those which the ruling classes are forced to concede by Direct Action.

The revolution gave the French another lesson. They saw how completely helpless were their intellectual leaders when it came to finding out about new forms of production which would secure for the workers their share and bring about the end of their exploitation by Capital. They saw this helplessness both in the Luxembourg Commission, which met between April and June 1848, and in the special Chamber chosen to study this question in 1849, on which over 100 Social Democratic Deputies sat. From this, they realized that workers themselves had to work out the main lines of the social revolution, on which they must travel if they are to be successful.

The use of direct action by Labor against Capital, and the necessity for workers themselves to work out the forms of economic organization with which to eliminate capitalist exploitation: these were the two main lessons received by the workers, especially in the two countries with the most developed industry.

When, then, in the years 1864/66 the old idea of Robert Owen was realized and an international worker's organization was set up, this new organization adopted both of the above fundamental principles. As the International Workers Association (IWA) had been brought into being by representatives of the British trade unions and French workers (mainly followers of Proudhon), who had attended the second World Exhibition in Paris, it proclaimed that the emancipation of the workers must be the task of the workers themselves and that from then on the capitalists would have to be fought with mass strikes, supported internationally.

Following on from this, the first two acts of the International were two such mass strikes, causing enormous agitation in Europe and a salutary fright for the middle class: a strike in Paris, supported by the British trade unions, the other in the Genoese building trade, supported by French and British workers.

In addition, congresses of the International workers no longer bothered with discussing nonsense with which nations were entertained by their rulers in parliamentary institutions. They discussed the fundamental question of the revolutionary reconstruction of society and set in motion the idea which since then has proved so fruitful—the idea of the General Strike. As to what political form society would take after the social revolution, the federations of the Latin countries openly stood against the idea of centralized states. They emphatically declared themselves in favor of an organization based on a federation of free communes and farming regions, which in this way would free themselves from capitalist exploitation and on this basis, on the basis of federal combination, form larger territorial and national units.

Both basic principles of modern Syndicalism, of direct action and the careful working out of new forms of social life, are based on trade union federations: from the beginning, both were the leading principles of the IWA.

Even them within the Association, however, there were two differing currents of opinion concerning political activity which divided the workers of different nations: Latin, and German.

The French within the International

were mainly supporters of Proudhon, whose leading idea was as follows: The removal of the existing bourgeois state apparatus, to be replaced by the workers own organization of trade unions, which will regulate and organize everything essential to society. It is the workers who have to organize the production of life's necessities, the fair and impartial exchange of all products of human labor, and their distribution and consumption. And if they do that, we will see that there will be very little left for the state to do. Production of everything needed, and a more equitable exchange and consumption of products, are problems which only the workers can solve. If they can do all this, what remains to be done by existing governments and their hierarchy of officials? Nothing that workers can't organize themselves.

But among the French founders of the International there were those who had fought for the Republic and for the Commune. They were insistent that political activity should not be ignored and that it is not unimportant for the proletarian whether they live under a monarchy, a Republic, or a commune. They knew from their own experience that the triumph of conservatives or of imperialists meant repression in all directions, and an enormous weakening of the power of workers to combat the aggressive politics of the capitalists. They were not indifferent to politics, but they refused to see an instrument for the liberation of the working class in electoral politics or successes, or in the whole to-ing and fro-ing of political parties. Accordingly, the French, Spanish, and Italian workers agreed to insert the following words into the statutes of the International: "Every political activity must be secondary to the economic."

Among British workers there were a number of Chartists who supported political struggle. And the Germans, unlike the French, did not yet have the experience of two republics. They believed in the coming parliament of the German Reich. Even Lasalle – as is now known – had some faith in a socialist Kaiser of the united Germany he saw rising.

Because of this, neither the British nor the Germans wanted to rule out parliamentary action, which they still believed in, and in the English and German texts of the same statutes inserted: "As a means, every political activity must be secondary to the economic."

Thus was resurrected the old idea of

trust in a bourgeois parliament.

After Germany had triumphed over France in the war of 1870-71 and 35,000 proletarians, the cream of the French working class, were murdered after the fall of the Commune by the armies of the bourgeoisie, and when the IWA had been banned in France, Marx and Engels and their supporters tried to re-introduce political activity into the International, in the form of workers candidates.

As a result, a split occurred in the International, which up to then had raised such high hopes among proletarians and caused such fright among the rich.

The federations of the Latin countries, of Italy, Spain, the Jura and East Belgium (and a small group of refugees from France) rejected the new course. They formed their own separated unions and since this time have developed more and more in the direction of revolutionary Syndicalism and Anarchism, while Germany took the lead in the development of the Social Democratic Party, all the more so after Bismarck introduced the universal right to vote in parliamentary elections following the victory in war of the newly established German Reich.

Forty years have now passed since this division in the International and we can judge the result. Later, we will analyze things in more detail but even now we can point to the complete lack of success during these 40 years of those who placed their faith in what they called the conquest of political power within the existing bourgeois state.

Instead of conquering this state, as they believed, they have been conquered by it. They are its tools, helping to maintain the power of the upper and middle class over the workers. They are the loyal tools of the Church, State, Capital and the monopoly economy.

But all across Europe and America we are seeing a new movement among the masses, a new force in the worker's movement, one which turns to the old principles of the International, of direct action and the direct struggle of the workers against capital, and workers are realizing that they alone must free themselves – not parliament.

Obviously, this is still not Anarchism. We go further. We maintain that the workers will only achieve their liberation when they rid themselves of the perception of centralization and hierarchy, and of the deception of State appointed officials who maintain law and order – law made by the rich directed against the poor, and order meaning the submission of the poor before rich. Until such fantasies and delusions have been thrown overboard, the emancipation of the workers will not be achieved.

But during theses 40 years anarchists, together with these workers who have taken their liberation into their own hands, making use of Direct Action as the preparatory means for the final battle of exploited Labor against – up to the present day – triumphant Capital, have fought against those who entertained the workers with fruitless electoral campaigns. All this time they have been busy among the working masses, to awaken in them the desire for working out the principles for the seizure of the docks, railways, mines, factories, fields and warehouses, by the unions, to be run no longer in the interests of a few capitalists but in the interest of the whole of society.

It has been shown how in England since the years 1820-30, and in France following the unsuccessful political revolution of 1848, the efforts of an important section of the workers were directed at fighting Capital using Direct Action, and with creating the necessary worker's organizations for this.

It has also been shown how, between 1866 and 1870, this idea was the most important within the newly established International Workers Association but also how, following the defeat of France by Germany in 1871 and the fall of the Paris Commune, political elements took the upper hand within the International through this collapse of its revolutionary forces and temporarily became the decisive factor in the worker's movement.

Since this time both currents have steadily developed in the direction of their own programs. Worker's parties were organized in all constitutional states and did everything in their power to increase the number of their parliamentary representatives as quickly as possible. From the very beginning it could be seen how, with representatives who chased after votes, the economic program would increasingly become less important; in the end being limited to complete the trivial limitations on the rights of employers, thereby giving the capitalist system new strength and helping to prolong the old order. At the same time, those socialist politicians who competed with the representatives of bourgeois radicalism for the capture of worker's votes helped, if against their intentions, to smooth the way for a victorious reaction across Europe.

Their whole ideology, the ideas and ideals which they spread among the masses, were focused on the one aim. They were convinced supporters of state centralization, opposed local autonomy and the independence of small nations and devised a philosophy of history to support their conclusions. They poured cold water on the hopes of the masses while preaching to them, in the name of "historical materialism", that no fundamental change in a socialist direction would be possible if the number of capitalists did not decrease through mutual competition. Completely outside their observations lay the fact which is so obvious in all industrialized countries today: that British, French, Belgian and other capitalists, by means of the ease with which they exploit countries which themselves have no developed industry, today control the labor of hundreds of millions of people in Eastern Europe, Asia, and Africa. The result is that the number of those people in the leading industrialized countries of Europe who live off the work of others doesn't grad-

ually decrease at all. Far from it. In fact, it increases at a constant and alarming rate. And
with the growth of this number, the number
of people with an interest in the capitulation
of the capitalist state system also increases.
Finally, those who speak loudest of political
agitation for the conquest of power in the existing states fiercely oppose anything which
could damage their chances of achieving political power. Anyone who dared to criticize
their parliamentary tactics was expelled from
international socialist congresses. They dis-
approved of strikes and later, when the idea
of the General Strike penetrated even their
own congresses, they fought the idea fiercely
with all means at their disposal.

Such tactics have been pursued for a full
40 years, but only today has it become clear
to everyone that workers throughout Europe
have had enough. With disgust, many workers have come to reject them. This is the reason we are now hearing so much about "Syndicalism".

However, during these 40 years the other current, that which advocates the direct
struggle of the working class against Capital,
has also grown and developed; it has developed despite government persecution from

all directions and in spite of denunciation by capitalist politicians. It would be interesting to plot the steady development of this current and to analyze its intellectual as well as personal connections with the social democratic parties on the one hand, and with the anarchists on the other. But now is not the time for publication of such work, all things given it is perhaps better that it has not yet been written. Attention would be turned to the influence of personalities, when it is to the influence of the major currents of modern thought and the growth of self-confidence among the workers of America and Europe, a self-confidence gained independently of intellectual leaders, to which special attention has to be directed in order to be able to write a real history of Syndicalism.

All that we now have to say about it is the bare facts that completely independently of the teachings of Socialists, where working masses were gathered together in the main industrial centers, that these masses maintained the tradition of their trade organizations from former times, organizing both openly and secretly, while all the time growing in strength, to curb the increasing exploitation and arrogance of the employers.

At the same time that the organized working masses grew larger and stronger, becoming aware of the main struggle which since the time of the great French revolution has been the true purpose of life of civilized peoples, their anti-capitalist tendencies became clearer and more certain.

During the last 40 years, years in which political leaders in different countries have used the widest possible means to try to prevent all worker's revolts and to suppress any of a threatening character, we have seen workers' revolts extend even further, becoming ever more powerful, and workers' aims expressed more and more clearly. Ever increasingly, they have lost the character of mere acts of despair; whenever we have contact with the workers, more and more we hear the prevailing opinion expressed, which can be summarized in the following few words: "Make room, gentlemen of industry! If you can't manage to run the Industries so that we can scrape a living and find in them a secure existence, then away with you! Away, if you are so short sighted and incapable of coming to a sensible understanding with one another over each new turn of production which promises you the greatest instant profit, that you must attack without regarding the harmfulness or usefulness of its products like a flock of sheep! Away with you, if you are incapable of building up your wealth other than with the preparation of endless wars, wasting a third of all goods produced by each nation in armaments useful only for robbing other robbers! Away. If from all the wonderful discoveries of modern science you have not learnt to gain your riches other than from the poverty to which a third of the population of the big towns and cities of our exceptionally rich countries are condemned! Away, if that is the only way you can run industry and trade! We workers will know better how to organize production, if only first we succeed in eradicating this capitalist pest!"

These were the ideas fought over and discussed in workers' households throughout the entire civilized world; they provided the fertile ground for the tremendous workers' revolts we have seen year after year in Europe and in the United States, in the form of strikes by dockers, rail workers, miners and mill workers, etc., until finally taking the form of the General Strike – soon growing into major struggles comparable with the powerful cycles of the force of nature, and next to which small battles in parliaments appear as a children's game.

While the Germans celebrated their ever growing electoral success with red flags and torchlit possessions, the experienced Western people's quietly set to work on a much more serious task: that of the internal organization of the workers. The ideas with which these last peoples occupied themselves were of a much more important nature. They asked themselves, "What will be the result of the inevitable worldwide conflict between Labor and Capital?" "What new forms of industrial life and social organization will this conflict create?"

And that is the true origin of the Syndicalist movement, which today's ignorant politicians have just discovered as something new to them.

To us anarchists this movement is nothing new. We welcomed the recognition of syndicalist trends in the program of the International Workers Association. We defended it, when it was attacked within the International by the German political revolutionaries who saw in this movement an obstacle to the capture of political power. We advised the workers of all nations to follow the example of the Spanish who had kept their trade union organizations in close contact with the sections of the International. Since this time we have followed all phases of the worker's movement with interest and know that whatever the coming clashes between Labor and Capital will be like, it will fall to the syndicalist movement to open the eyes of society towards the tasks owing to the producers of all wealth. It is the only movement which will show to thinking people a way out of the cul-de-sac into which the present development of capitalism has given our generation.

It goes without saying that anarchists have never imagined that it was they who had provided the syndicalist movement with its understanding of its tasks with regard to the reorganization of society. Never have they absurdly claimed to be the leaders of a great intellectual movement leading humanity in the direction of its progressive evolution. But what we can claim is to have recognized right from the beginning the immense importance of those ideas which today constitute the main aims of Syndicalism, ideas which in Britain have been developed by Godwin, Hodgkin, Grey and their successors, and in France by Proudhon: The idea that workers' organizations for production, distribution, and exchange, must take the place of existing capitalist exploitation and the state. And that it is the duty and the task of the workers' organizations to work out the new form of society.

Neither of these two fundamental ideas are our invention, nor anyone else's. Life itself has dictated them to nineteenth century civilization. It is now our duty to put them into reality. But we are proud that we understood and defended them in those dark years when social democratic politicians and pseudo-philosophies trampled them underfoot, and we are proud that we stand true to them, today as then.

REVOLUTIONARY
GOVERNMENT

———

I.

That the Governments at present existing ought to be abolished, so that Liberty, Equality, and Fraternity should no longer be empty words but become living realities, and that all forms of government as yet tried have only been so many forms of oppression, and ought to be replaced by a new form of grouping, so far all who have a brain and temperament ever so little revolutionary unanimously agree. In truth one does not need to be much of an innovator in order to arrive at this conclusion; the vices of the governments of today, and the impossibility of reforming them, are too evident to be hidden from the eyes of any reasonable observer. And as regards overturning governments it is well-known that at certain epochs that can be down without much difficulty; there are times when governments crumble to pieces almost of themselves, like houses of cards, before the breath of the people in revolt. That has been seen clearly seen clearly in 1848 and in 1870; and will soon be seen again.

To overturn a government — this for a revolutionary middle-class man is everything, for us it is only the beginning of the Social Revolution. The machine of the State once out of gear, the hierarchy of functionaries disorganized and not knowing in what direction to take a step, the soldiers having lost confidence in their officers — in a word the whole army of the defenders of capital once routed — then it is that the grand work of destruction of all the institutions which serve to perpetuate economic and political slavery will become ours. The possibility of living freely being attained, what will revolutionists do next?

To this question the Anarchists alone give the proper answer, "No Government, Anarchy" All the others say "A Revolutionary Government!" and they only differ as to the form to be given to that government. Some decide for a government elected by universal suffrage in the State or in the Commune;

others decide on a Revolutionary Dictature.

* * *

A Revolutionary Government! These are two words which sounds very strange in the ears of those who really understand what the Social Revolution means, and what a government means. The words contradict each other, destroy each other. We have seen of course many despotic governments — it is the essence of all government to take the side of the re-action against the Revolution, and to have a tendency toward despotism — but such a thing as a revolutionary government has never been seen, and the reason is that the Revolution — synonym of "disorder" of upsetting and overthrowing of venerated institutions in a few days, meaning the demolition by violence of the established forms of property, the destruction of castes, the rapid transformation of received ideas about morality, or rather about the hypocrisy which takes the place of it, individual liberty and freedom of action — is precisely the opposite, the very negation, of government, this being the synonym of "established order," of conservatism, of the maintenance of existing institutions, the negation of free initiative and individual action. And yet we continually hear this white blackbird spoken of, as if a "revolutionary government" were the simplest thing in the world, as common and as well known to all as Royalty, the Empire and the Papacy!

That the so-called revolutionists of the middle-class should preach this idea is nothing strange. We know well what they understand by Revolution. They understand by it a bolstering up of their republic, the taking possession by the so-called republicans of the lucrative employments reserved today for the Bonapartists or Royalists. It means at the most the divorce of Church and State, replaced by the concubinage of the two, and above all for that of the future administrators of these goods; perhaps it may mean the *referendum*, or some other political machinery of the same kind. But that revolutionary socialists should make themselves the apostles of such an idea — we can only explain by supposing one of two things. Either they are imbued with prejudices which they have imbibed without knowing it from literature and above all from history, written to suit middle-class ideas; and still possessed with the spirit of servility, product of ages of slavery, they cannot even imagine themselves free. Or else they do not really desire this Revolution which they have always on their lips, they would be content with a simple plastering up of present institutions, provided that they would secure power for themselves, leaving to the future to decide what they should do to satisfy "the beast" called the People. They only go against the Governors of the present time in order to take their places. With these people we care not to argue. We will then only speak to those who honestly deceive themselves.

Let us begin with the first of the two forms of "Revolutionary Government" which is advocated — the elected government.

* * *

The power of Royalty or some other we will suppose has just been overturned, the army of the defenders of capital is routed; everywhere there is fermentation, discussion of public affairs, everywhere a desire to march onward — new ideas arise, the necessity of important changes is perceived — it is necessary to act, it is necessary to begin without pity the work of demolition, in order to prepare the ground for the new life. But what do they propose to us to go? To convoke the people to elections, to elect at once a government and confide to it the work which we all of us, and each of us, should undertake of our own initiative.

This is what Paris did after the 18th of March 1871. "I will never forget," said a friend to us, "these delightful moments of deliverance." I came down from my upper chamber in the Latin Quarter to join that immense open-air club which filled the Boulevards from one end of Paris to the other. Everyone talked about public affairs; all mere personal preoccupations were forgotten; no more was thought of buying or selling; all felt ready body and soul to advance toward the future. Men of the middle-class even, carried away by the general enthusiasm saw with joy a new world opened up. "If it is necessary to make a social revolution," they said, "make it then. Put all things in common; we are ready for it." All the elements of the revolution were there. It was only necessary to set them to work. When I returned to my lodging at night I said to myself, "How fine is humanity after al,l but no one knew it; it has always been calumniated." Then came the elections, the members of the Commune were named — and then little by little the ardor of devotion, and the desire for action were extinguished. Everyone returned to his usual task saying to himself "Now we have an honest government, let it act for us" — What followed everyone knows.

Instead of acting for themselves, instead of marching forwards, instead of advancing in the direction of a new order of things, the people, confiding in their governors, entrusted to them the charge of taking the initiative — this was the first consequence of the inevitable result of elections. Let us see now what these governors did who were invested with the confidence of all.

* * *

Never were elections more free than those of March, 1871. The opponents of the Commune admit it themselves. Never was the great mass of electors more influenced with the desire to place in power the best men, men for the future, true revolutionists. And so they did. All well-known Revolutionists were elected by immense majorities; Jacobins Blanquists, Internationals, all the three revolutionary divisions were represented in the Council of the Commune. No election could give a better government.

But what was the result of it? Shut up in the City Mansion, charged to proceed after the forms established by preceding governments, these ardent revolutionists, these reformers found themselves smitten with incapacity and sterility. With all their good will and their courage they did not even know how to organize the defense of Paris. Of course people now blame the men, the individuals for this; but it was not the men who were the cause of this failure — it was the system carried out.

In fact universal suffrage, when it is quite free, can only produce, at best, an assembly which represents the average of the opinions which at the time are held by the mass of the people; and this average at the outbreak of the Revolution, has only a vague idea of the work to be accomplished, without understanding at all how they ought to undertake it. Ah, if the bulk of the nation, of the Commune, could only understand *before* the movement what was necessary to be done as soon as the government should be overturned! If this dream of the utopians of the chair could be realized we never would have had bloody revolutions; the will of the bulk of the nation once expressed the rest would submit to it with a good grace. But this is not how things are done. The Revolution bursts out long before a general understanding has been come to, and those who have a clear idea of what should be done the next day are only a very small minority. The great mass of the people have as yet only a general idea of the end which they wish realized, without knowing much how to advance toward that end, nor much confidence in the direction to follow. The practical solution will not be found, will not be made clear until the change will have already begun; it will be the product of the Revolution itself, of the people in action — or else it will be nothing, the brain of a few individuals being absolutely incapable of finding solutions which can only spring from the life of the people.

This is the situation which is reflected in the body elected by universal suffrage, even if it had not all the vices inherent in representative governments in general. The few men who represent the revolutionary idea of the epoch find themselves swamped among the representatives of the revolutionary schools of the past, and of the existing order of things. These men who would be so necessary among the people, particularly in the days of the Revolution, to so broadcast their ideas, to put the mass in movement, to demolish the institutions of the past — find themselves shut up in a Hall, vainly discussing how to wrest concessions from the moderated, and how to convert their enemies, while there is really only one way of inducing them to accept the new idea — namely to put it in execution. The government becomes a parliament with all the vices of a middle-class parliament. Far from being a "revolutionary" government it becomes the greatest obstacle to the Revolution, and at last the people finds itself compelled to put it out of the way, to dismiss those that but yesterday it acclaimed as its chosen. But it is not so easy to do so. The new government, which has hastened to organize a new administration in order to extend its domination and make itself to be obeyed, does not understand giving up so easily. Jealous of maintaining its power, it clings to it with all the energy of an institution which has not yet had time to fall into senile decay. It decides to oppose force with force, and there is only one means then to dislodge it, namely, to take up arms, to make another revolution in order to dismiss those in whom the people had placed all their hopes.

There you see the Revolution divided against itself! After losing precious time in delays, it now loses its strength in intestine divisions between the friends of the new government, and those who see the necessity of dissolving it. And all this happens because it has not been understood that a new life requires new forms; that it is not by clinging to ancient forms that a revolution can be carried out! All this for not having understood the incompatibility of revolution and government, for not having seen that the one is, under whatever form it presents itself, the *negation* of the other, and that outside of Anarchy there is no such thing as revolution.

It is just the same with regard to that other form of "revolutionary government" so often extolled — a Revolutionary Dictature.

II.

The dangers to which the Revolution is exposed when it allows itself to be controlled by an elected government, are so evident that a whole school of Revolutionists renounce entirely the idea of it. They understand that it is impossible for a people in insurrection to give themselves, by means of elections, any government but one that represents the past, and which must be like leaden shoes on the feet of the people, above all when it is necessary to accomplish that immense regeneration, economic, political and moral which we understand by the Social Revolution. They renounce then the idea of "legal" government at least during that period which is a revolt against legality, and they advocate a "revolutionary dictatorship."

"The party" they say "which will have overturned the government will take the place of it of course. It will seize upon power and proceed in a revolutionary manner. It will take the measures necessary to secure the success of the insurrection; it will demolish the old institutions; it will organize the defense of the country. As for those who will not recognize its authority, why the guillotine will settle them, whether they belong to the people or the middle-class, if they refuse to obey the orders necessary for the advance of the Revolution — The guillotine still in action! See how these budding Robespierres argue, who know nothing of the grand epic of the century but its period of decline, men who have never learned anything about it except from speeches of the hangers-on of the republic.

* * *

For us Anarchists the dictature of an individual or of a party (at bottom the very same thing) has been finally condemned. We know that Revolution and Government are incompatible; one must destroy the other, no matter what name is given to government, whether dictature, royalty, or parliament. We know that what makes the strength and the truth of our party is contained in this fundamental formula — "Nothing good or durable can be done except by the free initiative of the people, and every government tends to destroy it;" and so the very best among us, if their ideas had not to pass through the crucible of the popular mind, before being put into execution, and if they should become masters of that formidable machine — the government — and could thus act as they chose, would become in a week fit only for the gallows. We know whither every dictature leads, even the best intentioned—namely to the death of all revolutionary movement. We know also in fine, that this idea of dictature is never anything more than a sickly product of governmental fetish-worship, which like religious fetish worship has always served to perpetuate slavery.

But we do not now address ourselves to Anarchists. We speak to those governmental Revolutionists, who, led astray by the prejudices of their education, honestly deceive themselves, and ask nothing better than to discuss the question. We therefore speak to them from their own point of view.

* * *

And to being with one general observation; those who preach dictature do not in general perceive that in sustaining this prejudice they only prepare the way for those who later on will cut their throats. There is however one word of Robespierre's which his admirers would do well to remember. *He* did not deny the dictature in principle; but "have good care about it" he answered abruptly to Mandar when he spoke to him of it, *"Brissot would be the Dictator!"* Yes, Brissot, the crafty girondin, deadly enemy of the leveling tendencies of the people, furious defender of property (though he once called it theft) Brissot, who would coolly have consigned to the Abbaye Prison Hebert, Marat, and all the moderate Jacobins!

Now this was said in 1792! And this time France had already been three years in Revolution! In fact Royalty no longer existed, it only awaited its death stroke; the feudal regime was actually abolished. And yet even at this time, when the Revolution rolled its waves untrammeled, it was still the counter-revolutionist Brissot who had the best chance to be made dictator! And who would it have been previously, in 1789? Mirabeau is the man would have been acknowledged as the head of the government! The man who made a bargain with the king to sell to him his eloquence — this is the man who would have been thrust into power at this time, if the insurgent people ad not imposed its sovereignty sustained by its pikes, and if it had not proceeded by *the accomplished facts* of the Jacquerie, in making illusory every government constituted at Paris or in the departments.

But governmental prejudice blinds so thoroughly those who speak of dictature, that they prefer the dictature of a new Brissot or a Napoleon to abandoning the idea of giving another master to men who are breaking the chains of their slavery!

* * *

The secret societies of the time of the

Restoration and Louis-Philippe contributed powerfully to maintain this prejudice of dictature. The middle-class Republicans of the time aided by the workers made a long series of conspiracies, with the object of overturning Royalty and proclaiming the Republic. Not understanding the profound change that would have to be effected in France before even a republican regime could be established, they imagined that by means of a vast conspiracy, they would some day overturn Royalty, take possession of power and proclaim the Republic. For more than thirty years these secret societies never ceased to work with a devotion unlimited, and a heroic courage and perseverance. If the Republic resulted from the insurrection of 1848, it was thanks to these societies, and thanks to the propaganda by deed made by them for thirty years.

Without their noble efforts the Republic would, up the present, have been impossible.

* * *

The end they had in view was to get possession of power themselves and to install a republican dictature. But of course they never succeeded. As ever, from the very nature of things, a conspiracy could not overturn Royalty. The conspirators had indeed prepared the way for its fall. They had spread widely the republican idea; their martyrs had made it the ideal of the people. But the final effort which definitely overturned the king of the bourgeoisie was much greater and stronger than any that could come from a secret society; it came from the mass of the people.

The result is known. The party, which had prepared the way for the fall of royalty, found itself thrust aside from the steps of the Government House. Others, too prudent to run the risks of conspiracy, but better known, more moderate also, lying in wait for the opportunity of grasping power, took the place which the conspirators hoped to conquer at the point of they bayonet. Journalists, lawyers, good talkers who worked hard to make a name for themselves while the true republicans forged weapons or expired in jail, took permission of power. Some of them, already well known were acclaimed by the people; others pushed themselves forward and were accepted because their name represented nothing more than a program of agreement with everybody.

It is useless to tell us that this happened

because of a want or practical spirit in the party action, and that other will be able to do better in future — No, a thousand times no! It is a law as immutable as that which governs the movement of the stars, that the party of action must be thrown aside, and the intriguers and talkers seize upon power. They are always better known to the great mass that makes the final effort. They get more votes, because with of without voting papers, by acclamation or by the ballot box, at the bottom it is always a kind of tacit election which is made in such cases by acclamation. They are acclaimed by everybody and above all by the enemies of the Revolution, who prefer to put forward nobodies, and thus by acclamation those men are accepted as rulers who are really either enemies of the movement or indifferent toward it.

The man who more than any other was the incarnation of this system of conspiracy, the man who by a life spent in prison for his devotion to this system, on the eve of his death uttered these words, which of themselves make an entire program — "Neither God nor Master!"

III.

To imagine that a government can be overturned by a secret society, and that the secret society can take its place, is an error into which have fallen all the revolutionary organizations which sprang to life in the bosom of the republican middle-class since 1820. And yet facts abound which prove what an error it is. What devotion, what abnegation, what perseverance was not displayed by the republican secret societies of the Young Italy Party! And yet all this immense work, all these sacrifices made by the youth of Italy, before which even those of the Russian Revolutionary youth pale, all the corpses piled up in the casemated of Austrian fortresses, and under the knife and bullets of the executioner — all this only brought into power the crafty, robbing middle-class and royalty!

It was the same in Russia. It is difficult to find in history a secret organization which has obtained, with such limited means, results so immense as those attained by the Russian youth, or which has shown such energy or such powerful activity as their executive committee. It has shaken a colossus which appeared invulnerable — Czarism; and it has rendered autocratic government henceforth impossible in Russia. And still it is only simple fools who imagine that the Executive Committee will get into power when the crown of Alexander III is dragged in the more. Other men — the prudent ones, who strove to make a name for themselves while the revolutionists laid and spring mine or perished in Siberia, these others — the intriguers, the talkers, the lawyers, the journalists who now and again shed a few tears very soon dried up, on the tomb of the heroes, and make believe they are friends of the people — these are the men who will come and take the place left vacant by the Government, and will shout "stand back" to those "unknown persons" who will have prepared they way for the Revolution.

* * *

It is inevitable, it cannot be otherwise. For it is not secret societies nor even Revolutionary organizations that can give finishing blown to governments. Their functions, their historic mission is to prepare men's minds for the Revolution and then when men's minds are prepared and external circumstances are favorable, the final rush is made, not by the group that initiated the movement, but by the mass of the people altogether outside of the society. On the 31st of August, Paris was deaf to the appeals of Blanqui. Four day later he proclaimed the fall of the government; but then the Blanquists were no longer the initiators of the movement; it was the people, the millions who dethrone the man of December, and proclaimed the humbugs whose names for two hears had resounded in their ears. When a Revolution is ready to burst out, when the movement is felt in the air, when its success is already *certain*, then a thousand new men, on whom the organization has never exercised any direct influence, come and join the movement, like birds of prey coming to the field of battle to feed on the victims. These help to make the final effort, but it is not in the ranks of the sincere and irreconcilable conspirators, it is among the men on the fence that they look for their leaders. The conspirators who still are possessed with the prejudice of a dictature work then unconsciously to put into power their own enemies.

* * *

But if all this that we have just said is true with regard to political revolutions or rather outbreaks, it is much more true with regard to the Revolution we desire — the Social Revolution. To allow any government to be established, a strong and recognized power, it is to paralyze the work of the Revolution at once. The good that this government could do is nil, and the evil immense.

For what is it we have on hand? What do we understand by Revolution? It is not a simple change of governors. It is the taking possession by the people of all social wealth. It is the abolition of all the forces which have so long hampered the development of Humanity. But is it by decrees emanating from a government that this immense economic revolution can be accomplished? We have seen in the past century the Polish revolutionary dictator Kosciusko decree the abolition of personal servitude, yet the servitude continued to exist for eighty years after this decree. We have the Convention, the omnipotent Convention, the terrible Convention as its admirers call it, decree the equal division *per head* of all he Communal lands taken back from the nobles. Like so many other this decree remained a dead letter because in order to carry it out it was necessary that the proletarians of the rural districts should make an entirely new Revolution, and Revolutions are not made by the force of decrees. In order that the taking possession of social wealth should become an accomplished fact it is necessary that the people should have their hands free, that they would shake off the slavery to which they are too much habituated, that they act according to their own will, and march forward without waiting for orders from anyone. And it is this very thing which a dictature would prevent however well integrated it might be, while it would be incapable of advancing in the slightest degree the march of the Revolution.

* * *

But if government, were it even an ideal Revolutionary government, creates no new force and is of no use whatever in the work of demolition which we have to accomplish, still less can we count on it for the work of reorganization which must follow that of demolition. The economic change which will result from the Social Revolution will be so immense and so profound, it must so change all the relations based today on property and exchange, that it is impossible for one or any individual to elaborate the different social forms, which must spring up in the society of the future. This elaboration of new social forms can only be made by the collective work of the masses. To satisfy the immense variety of conditions and needs which will spring up as soon as private property shall be abolished, it is necessary to have the collective suppleness of mind of the whole people. Any authority external to it will only be an obstacle, only a trammel on the organic labor which must be accomplished, and beside that a source of discord and hatred.

But it is full time to give up this illusion so often roved false and often dearly paid for, of a *Revolutionary* Government. It is time to admit, once and for all, this political axiom that a *government cannot be* revolutionary. People talk of the convention, but let us not forget that the few measures taken by the Convention, little revolutionary though they were, were only the sanction of action accomplished by the people who at the time trampled under foot all governments. As Victor Hugo has said, Danton pushed forward Robespierre, Marat watched and pushed on Danton, and Marat himself was pushed on by Cimourdain — this personification of the clubs of wild enthusiasts and rebels. Like all the governments that preceded it and followed it, the Convention was only a drag on the action of the people.

* * *

The facts which history teach us are so conclusive in this respect, the impossibility of a Revolutionary Government and the injurious effect of that which is called by the name are so evident, that it would seem difficult to explain the determination with which a certain school calling itself Socialist maintains the idea of a government. But the explanation is very simple. It is that Socialists, though they say they are the followers of this school, have an entirely different conception from ours of the Revolution which we have to accomplish. For them, as for the idle-class Radicals, the Social Revolution is rather an affair of the future about which we have not to think much at present. What they dream of in their inmost thoughts, though they don't dare to confess it, is something entirely different. It is the installation of a government like that of Switzerland or the United States, making some attempts at appropriation in favor of the State of what they call "public services." It is something after the ideal of Bismark. It is a compromise made in advance between the Socialistic aspirations of the masses and the series of the middle class. They would indeed wish the appropriation to be complete, but they have not courage to attempt it; so they put it off to the next century, and before the battle they enter into negotiation with the enemy.

For us who understand that the moment is near for giving a mortal blow to the middle-class, that the time is not far off when the people will be able to lay their hands on all social wealth and reduce the class of exploiters to a state of impotence, for us I say there can be no hesitation in the matter. We fling ourselves body and soul into the *Social* Revolution, and as on the road we follow, a government, whatever may be its device, is an obstacle, we will sweep from our path all ambitious men, however they shall come to thrust themselves upon us as governors of our destinies.

Away with Governments; make room for the People, and Anarchy!

THE COMING ANARCHY

There was a time when a family engaged
in agriculture, and, supported by a few do-
mestic trades, could consider the corn they
raised and the plain woolen cloth they wove
as production of their own and nobody else's
labor. Even then, such a view was not quite
correct: there were forests cleared and roads
built by common efforts; and even then the
family had continually to apply for communal
help, as it is still the case in so many village
communities. But now, under the extremely
interwoven state of industry, of which each
branch supports all others, such the individualistic view can be held no more. If the iron
trade and the cotton industry of this country
have reached so high a degree of development, they have done so owing to the par-
allel growth of the railway system; to an in-

crease of knowledge among both the skilled engineers and the mass of the workmen; to a certain training in organization slowly developed among British producers; and, above all, to the world trade, which has itself grown up thanks to works executed thousands of miles away. The Italians who died from cholera in digging the Suez Canal, or from "tunnel-disease" in the St. Gothard Tunnel, have contributed as much towards the enrichment of this country as the British girl who is prematurely growing old in serving a machine at Manchester; and this girl is much as the engineer who made a labor-saving improvement in our machinery. How can we pretend to estimate the exact part of each of them in the riches accumulated around us?

We may admire the inventive genius or the organizing capacities of an iron lord; but we must recognize that all his genius and energy would not realize one-tenth of what they realize here if they were spent dealing with Mongolian shepherds or Siberian peasants instead of British workmen, British engineers, and trustworthy managers. An English millionaire who succeeded in giving a powerful impulse to a branch of home industry was asked the other day what were, in his opinion, the real causes of his success.

His answer was, "I always sought out the right man for a given branch of concern, and I left him full independence — maintaining, of course, for myself the general supervision."

"Did you never fail to find such men?" was the next question.

"Never."

"But in the new branches which you introduced you wanted a number of new inventions."'

"No doubt; we spend thousands in buying patents."

This little colloquy sums up, in my opinion, the real case of those industrial undertakings, which are quoted by the advocates of "an adequate remuneration of individual efforts" in the shape of millions bestowed on the managers of prosperous industries. It shows how far the efforts are really "individual." Leaving aside the thousand conditions which sometimes permit a man to show, and sometimes prevent him from showing, his capacities to their full extent, it might be asked in how far the same capacities could bring out the same results, if the very same employer could find no inventions that were not stimulated by the mechanical turn of mind of so many inhabitants of this country. British industry is the work of the British nation — nay, of Europe and India taken together — not of a spate of individuals.

While holding this synthetic view on production, the anarchists cannot consider, like the collectivists, that a remuneration which would be proportionate to the hours of labor spent by each person in the production of riches may be an ideal, or even an approach to an ideal, society. Without entering here into a discussion as to how far the exchange value of each merchandise is really measured now by the amount of labor necessary for its production — a separate study must be devoted to the subject — we must say that the collectivist ideal seems to us merely unrealizable in a society which would be brought to consider the necessities for production as a common property. Such a society would be compelled to abandon the wage-system altogether. It appears impossible that the mitigated individualism of the collectivist school could co-exist which the partial communism implied by holding land and machinery in common — unless imposed by a powerful government, much more powerful than all those of our own times. The present wage-system has grown up from the appropriation of the necessities for production by the few; it was a necessary condition for the growth of the present capitalist production; and it cannot outlive it, even if an attempt be made to pay to the worker the full value of his produce, and money be substituted by hours of labor checks. Common possession of the necessaries for production implies that common enjoyment of the fruits of the common production; and we consider that an equitable organization of society can only arise when every wage-system is abandoned, and when everybody, contributing for the common wellbeing to the full extent of his capacities, shall enjoy also from the common stock of society to the fullest possible of his needs.

We maintain, moreover, not only that communism is a desirable state of society, but that the growing tendency of modern society is precisely towards communism — free communism — notwithstanding the seemingly contradictory growth of individualism. In the growth of individualism (especially during the last three centuries) we merely see the endeavors of the individual towards emancipating himself from the steadily growing powers of Capital and the State.

But side by side with this growth we see also, throughout history up to our own times, the latent struggle of the producers of wealth for maintaining the partial communism of old, as well as for reintroducing communist principles in a new shape, as soon as favorable conditions permit it. As soon as the communes of the tenth, eleventh, and twelfth centuries were enabled to start their own independent life, they gave a wide extension to work in common, to trade in common, and to a partial consumption in common. All this has disappeared; but the rural commune fights a hard struggle to maintain its old features, and it succeeds in maintaining them in many places of Eastern Europe, Switzerland, and even France and Germany; while new organizations, based on the same principles, never fail to grow up as soon as it is possible. Notwithstanding the egotistic turn given to public mind by the merchant-production of our century, the communist tendency is continually reasserting itself and trying to make its way into the public life. The penny bridge disappears before the public bridge; so also the road which formerly had to be paid for its use. Museums, free libraries, and free public schools; parks and pleasure grounds; paved and lighted streets, free for everybody's use; water supplied to private dwellings, with a growing tendency towards disregarding the exact amount of it used by the individual; tramways and railways which have already begun to introduce the season ticket or the uniform tax, and will surely go much further on this line when they are no longer private property: all these are tokens showing in which direction further progress is to be expected.

It is putting the wants of the individual above the valuation of the services he has rendered, or might render, to society; it is in considering society as a whole, so intimately connected together that a service rendered to any individual is a service rendered to the whole society. The librarian of the British Museum does not ask the reader what have been his previous services to society, he simply gives him the book he requires; and for a uniform fee, a scientific Society leaves its gardens and museums at the free disposal of each member . The crew of a lifeboat do not ask whether the men of a distressed ship are entitled to be rescued at a risk of life; and the Prisoners' Aid Society do not inquire what the released prisoner is worth. Here are men in need of service; they are fellow men, and no further rights are required. And if this very city, so egotistic today, be visited by a public calamity — let it be besieged, for example, like Paris in 1871, and experience during the siege a want of food — this very same city would be unanimous in proclaiming that the first needs to be satisfied are those of the children and old, no matter what services they may render or have rendered to society. And it would take care of the active defenders of the city, whatever the degrees of gallantry displayed by each of them. But, this tendency already existing, nobody will deny, I suppose, that, in proportion as humanity is relieved from its hard struggle for life, the same tendency will grow stronger. If our productive powers be fully applied for increasing the stock of the staple necessities for life; if a modification of the present conditions of property increased the number of producers by all those who are not producers of wealth now; and if manual labor reconquered its place of honor in society — all this decuplating our production and rendering labor easier and more attractive — the communist tendencies already existing would immediately enlarge their sphere of application.

Taking all that into account, and still more the practical aspects of the question as to how private property might become common property, most of the anarchists maintain that the very next step to be made by society, as soon as the present regime of property undergoes a modification, will be in a communist sense. We are communists. But our communism is not that of either the Phalanstere or the authoritarian school: it is anarchist communism, communism without government, free communism. It is a synthesis of the two chief aims prosecuted by humanity since the dawn of its history — economical freedom and political freedom.

I have already said that anarchy means no-government. We know well that the word 'anarchy' is also used in the current language as synonymous with disorder. But that meaning of 'anarchy' being a derived one, implies at least two suppositions. It implies, first, that whenever there is no government there is disorder; and it implies, moreover, that order, due to a strong government and a strong police, is always beneficial. Both implications, however, are anything but proved. There is plenty of order — we should say, of harmony — in many bunches of human activity where the government, happily, does not interfere. As to the beneficial effects of order, the kind of order that reigned at Naples under the Bourbons surely was not preferable to some disorder started by Garibaldi; while the Protestants of the this country will probably say that the good deal of disorder made by Luther was preferable, at any rate, to the order which reigned under the Pope. As to the proverbial "order," which was once "restored at Warsaw," there are, I suppose, no two opinions about it. While all agree that harmony is always desirable, there is no such unanimity about order, and still less about the "order" which is supposed to reign on our modern societies; so that we have no objection whatever to the use of the word "anarchy" as a negation of what has been often described as order.

By taking for our watchword anarchy, in its sense of no-government, we intend to express a pronounced tendency of human society. In history we see that precisely those epochs when small parts of humanity broke down the power of their rulers and reassumed their freedom were epochs of the greatest progress, economical and intellectual. Be it the growth of the free cities, whose unrivalled monuments — free work of free associations of workers — still testify of the revival of mind and of the well-being of the citizen; be it the great movement which gave birth to the Reformation — those epochs witnessed the greatest progress when the individual recovered some part of his freedom. And if we carefully watch the present development of civilized nations, we cannot fail to discover in it a marked and ever-growing movement towards limiting more and more the sphere of action of government, so as to leave more and more liberty to the initiative of the individual. After having tried all kinds of government, and endeavoring to solve the insoluble problem of having a government "which might compel the individual to obedience, without escaping itself from obedience to collectively," humanity is trying now to free itself from the bonds of any government whatever, and to respond to its needs of organization by the free understanding between individuals prosecuting the same common aims. Home Rule, even for the smallest territorial unity or group, becomes a growing need; free agreement is becoming a substitute for the law; and free co-operation a substitute for the governmental guardianship. One after the other those functions which were considered as the functions of government during the last two centuries are disputed; society moves better the less it is governed. And the more we study the advance made in this direction, as well as the inadequacy of governments to fulfill the expectations laid in them, the more we are bound to conclude that Humanity, by steadily limiting the functions of government, is marching towards reducing them finally to nil; and we already foresee a state of society where the liberty of the individual will be limited by no laws, no bonds — by nothing else by his own social habits and the necessity, which everyone feels, of finding co-operation, support, and sympathy among his neighbors.

Of course, the no-government ethics will meet with at least as many objectives as the no-capital economics. Our minds have been so nurtured is prejudices as to the providential functions of government that anarchist ideas must be received with distrust. Our whole education, since childhood up to the grave, nurtures the belief in the necessity of a government and its beneficial effects. Systems of philosophy have been elaborated to support this view; history has been written from this standpoint; theories of law have been circulated and taught for the same purpose. All politics are based on the same principles, each politician saying to the people he wants to support him: "Give me the governmental power; I will, I can, relieve you from the hardships of your present life." All our education is permeated with the same teachings. We may open any book of sociology, history, law, or ethics: everywhere we find government, its organization, its deeds, playing so prominent a part that we grow accustomed to suppose that the State and the political men are everything; that there is nothing behind the big statesmen. The same teachings are daily repeated in the Press. Whole columns are filled up with minutest records of parliamentary debates, of movements of political persons; and, while reading these columns, we too often forget that there is an immense body of men — man-kind, in fact — growing and dying, living in happiness or sorrow, laboring and consuming, thinking and creating, besides those few men whose importance has been so swollen up as to overshadow humanity.

And yet, if we revert from the printed matter to our real life, and cast a broad glance on society as it is, we struck with the infinitesimal part played by government in our life. Millions of human beings live and die without having had anything to do with government. Every day millions of transactions are made without the slightest interference of government; and those who enter into agreements have not the slightest intention of breaking bargains. Nay, those agreements which are not protected by government (those of the Exchange, or card debts) are perhaps better kept than any others. The simple habit of keeping his word, the desire of not losing confidence, are quite sufficient in the immense overwhelming majority of cases to enforce the keeping of agreements. Of course, it may be said that there is still the government which might enforce them if necessary. But not to speak of the numberless cases which even could not be brought before a court, everybody who has the slightest acquaintance with trade will undoubtedly confirm the assertion that, if there were not so strong a feeling of honor to keep agreements, trade itself would become utterly impossible. Even those merchants and manufacturers who feel not the slightest remorse when poisoning their customers with all kinds of abominable drugs, duly labeled, even they also keep their commercial agreements. But, if such a relative morality as commercial honesty exists now, under the present conditions, when enrichment is the chief motive, the same feeling will further develop very fast as soon as robbing somebody of the fruits of his labor is no longer the economical basis of our life.

PRISONS:
UNIVERSITIES OF CRIME

———

Leaving aside the great question of "Crime and Punishment" which occupies now so many prominent lawyers and sociologists, I shall limit my remarks to the question: "Are prisons answering their purpose, which is that of diminishing the number of antisocial acts?"

To this question, every unprejudiced person who has a knowledge of prisons from the inside will certainly answer by an emphatic No. On the contrary, a serious study of the subject will bring everyone to the conclusion that the prisons — the best as much as the worst — are breeding places of criminality; that they contribute to render the antisocial acts worse and worse; that they are, in a word, the High Schools, the Universities of what is known as Crime.

Prisons

Of course, I do not mean that everyone who has been once in a prison will return to it. There are thousands people sent every year to prison by mere accident. But I maintain that the effect of a couple of years of life in a prison — from the very fact of its being a prison — is to increase in the individual those defects which brought him before a law court. These causes, being the love of risk, the dislike of work (due to an immense majority of cases to the want of a thorough knowledge of a trade), the despise of society with its injustice and hypocrisy, the want of physical energy, and the lack of will — all these causes will be aggravated by detention in a jail.

Five-and-twenty years ago, when I developed this idea in a book, now out of print (*In Russian and French Prisons*), I supported it by an examination of the facts revealed in France by an inquest made as to the numbers of *recidivistes* (second offense prisoners). The result of this inquest was that from two fifths to one half of all persons brought before the assizes and two fifths of all brought before the police courts had already been kept once or twice in a jail. The very tame figure of forty percent was found in this country; while according to Michael Davitt, as much as ninety-five percent of all those who are kept in penal servitude have previously received prison education.

A little reflection will show that things cannot be otherwise. A prison has, and must have, a degrading effect on its inmates. Take a man freshly brought to a jail. The moment he enters the house he is no more a human being. He is "Number So and So." He must have no more a will of his own. They put him in a fool's dress to underline his degradation. They deprive him of every intercourse with those towards who he may have an attachment and thus exclude the action of the only element which could have a good effect upon him.

Then he is put to labor, but not to a labor that might help to his moral improvement. Prison work is made to be an instrument of base revenge. What must the prisoner think of the intelligence of these "pillars of society" who pretend by such punishments to "reform" the prisoners?

In the French prisons the inmates are given some sort of useful and paid work. But even this work is paid at a ridiculously low scale, and, according to the prison authorities, it cannot be paid otherwise. Prison work, they say, is inferior slave work. The result is that the prisoner begins to hate his work, and finishes by saying, "The real thieves are not we, but those who keep us in."

The prisoner's brain is thus working over and over again upon the idea of the injustice of a society which pardons and often respects such swindlers as so many company promoters are, and wickedly punishes him, simply because he was not cunning enough. And the moment he is out he takes his revenge by some offense very often much graver than his first one. Revenge breeds revenge.

The revenge that was exercised upon him he exercises upon society. Every prison, because it is a prison, destroys the physical energy of its inmates. It acts upon them far worse than an Arctic wintering. The want of fresh air, the monotony of existence, especially the want of impressions, take all energy out of the prisoner and produce that craving for stimulants (alcohol, coffee) which Miss Allen spoke so truthfully the other day at the Congress of the British Medical Association. And finally, while most antisocial acts can be traced to a weakness of will, the prison education is directed precisely towards killing every manifestation of will.

Worse than that. I seriously recommend to prison reformers the *Prison Memoirs* of Alexander Berkman, who was kept for fourteen years in an American jail and has told with great sincerity his experience. One will see from this book how every honest feeling must be suppressed by the prisoner, if he does not decide never to go out of this hell.

What can remain of a man's will and good intentions after five or six years of such an education? And where can he go after his release, unless he returns to the very same chums whose company has brought him to the jail? They are the only ones who will receive him as an equal. But when he joins them he is sure to return to the prison in a very few months. And so he does. The jailers know it well.

I am often asked — What reforms of prison I should propose; but now, as twenty-five years ago, I really do not see how prisons could be reformed. They must be pulled down. I might say, or course: "Be less cruel, be more thoughtful of what you do." But that would come to this: "Nominate a Pestalozzi as Governor in each prison, and sixty more Pestalozzis as warders," which would be absurd. But nothing short of that would help.

So the only thing I could say to some quite well-intentioned Massachusetts prison officials who came once to ask my advice was this: If you cannot obtain the abolition of the prison system, then never accept a child or a youth in your prison. If you do so, it is manslaughter. And then, after having learned by experience what prisons are, refuse to be jailers and never be tired to say that prevention of crime is the only proper way to combat it. Healthy municipal dwellings at cost price, education in the family and at school — of the parents as well as the children; the learning by every boy and girl of a trade; communal and professional cooperation; societies for all sorts of pursuits; and, above all, idealism developed in the youths the longing after what is lifting human nature to higher interests.

This will achieve what punishment is absolutely incapable to do.

THE SPIRIT OF REVOLT

There are periods in the life of human society when revolution becomes an imperative necessity, when it proclaims itself as inevitable. New ideas germinate everywhere, seeking to force their way into the light, to find an application in life; everywhere they are opposed by the inertia of those whose interest it is to maintain the old order; they suffocate in the stifling atmosphere of prejudice and traditions. The accepted ideas of the constitution of the State, of the laws of social equilibrium, of the political and economic interrelations of citizens, can hold out no longer against the implacable criticism which is daily undermining them whenever occasion arises — in drawing room as in cabaret, in the writings of philosophers as in daily conversation. Political, economic, and social institutions are crumbling; the social structure, having become uninhabitable, is hindering, even preventing, the development of the seeds which are being propagated within its damaged walls and being brought forth around them.

The need for a new life becomes apparent. The code of established morality, that which governs the greater number of people in their daily life, no longer seems sufficient. What formerly seemed just is now felt to be a crying injustice. The morality of yesterday is today recognized as revolting immorality. The conflict between new ideas and old traditions flames up in every class of society, in every possible environment, in the very bosom of the family. The son struggles against his father, he finds revolting what his father has all his life found natural; the daughter rebels against the principles which her mother has handed down to her as the result of long experience. Daily, the popular conscience rises up against the scandals which breed amidst the privileged and the leisured, against the crimes committed in the name of the *law of the stronger*, or in order to maintain these privileges. Those who long for the triumph of justice, those who would put new ideas into practice, are soon forced to recognize that the realization of their generous, humanitarian and regenerating ideas cannot take place in a society thus constituted; they perceive the necessity of a revolutionary whirlwind which will sweep away all this rottenness, revive sluggish hearts with its breath, and bring to mankind that spirit of devotion, self-denial, and heroism, without which society sinks through degradation and vileness into complete disintegration.

In periods of frenzied haste toward wealth, of feverish speculation and of crisis, of the sudden downfall of great industries and the ephemeral expansion of other branches of production, of scandalous fortunes amassed in a few years and dissipated as quickly, it becomes evident that the economic institutions which control production and exchange are far from giving to society the prosperity which they are supposed to guarantee; they produce precisely the opposite result. Instead of order they bring forth chaos; instead of prosperity, poverty and insecurity; instead of reconciled interests, war; a perpetual war of the exploiter against the worker, of exploiters and of workers among themselves. Human society is seen to be splitting more and more into two hostile camps, and at the same time to be subdividing into thousands of small groups waging merciless war against each other. Weary of these wars, weary of the miseries which they cause, society rushes to seek a new organization; it clamors loudly for a complete remodeling of the system of property ownership, of production, of exchange and all economic relations which spring from it.

The machinery of government, entrusted with the maintenance of the existing order, continues to function, but at every turn of its deteriorated gears it slips and stops. Its working becomes more and more difficult, and the dissatisfaction caused by its defects grows continuously. Every day gives rise to a new demand. "Reform this," "reform that," is heard from all sides. "War, finance, taxes, courts, police, everything must be remodeled, reorganized, established on a new basis," say the reformers. And yet all know that it is impossible to make things over, to remodel anything at all because everything is interrelated; everything would have to be remade at once; and how can society be remodeled when it is divided into two openly hostile camps? To satisfy the discontented would be only to create new malcontents.

Incapable of undertaking reforms, since this would mean paving the way for revolution, and at the same time too impotent to be frankly reactionary, the governing bodies apply themselves to half-measures which can satisfy nobody, and only cause new dissatisfaction. The mediocrities who, in such transition periods, undertake to steer the ship of State, think of but one thing: to enrich themselves against the coming *débâcle*. Attacked from all sides, they defend themselves awkwardly, they evade, they commit blunder upon blunder, and they soon succeed in cutting the last rope of salvation; they drown the prestige of the government in ridicule, caused by their own incapacity.

Such periods demand revolution. It becomes a social necessity; the situation itself is revolutionary.

* * *

When we study in the works of our greatest historians the genesis and development of vast revolutionary convulsions, we generally find under the heading, "The Cause of the Revolution," a gripping picture of the situation on the eve of events. The misery of the people, the general insecurity, the vexatious measures of the government, the odious scandals laying bare the immense vices of society, the new ideas struggling to come to the surface and repulsed by the incapacity of the supporters of the former régime, — nothing is omitted. Examining this picture, one arrives at the conviction that the revolution was indeed inevitable, and that there was no other way out than by the road of insurrection.

Take, for example, the situation before 1789 as the historians picture it. You can almost hear the peasant complaining of the salt tax, of the tithe, of the feudal payments, and vowing in his heart an implacable hatred towards the feudal baron, the monk, the monopolist, the bailiff. You can almost see the citizen bewailing the loss of his municipal liberties, and showering maledictions upon the king. The people censure the queen; they are revolted by the reports of ministerial action, and they cry out continually that the taxes are intolerable and revenue payments exorbitant, that crops are bad and winters hard, that provisions are too dear and the monopolists too grasping, that the village lawyer devours the peasant's crops and the village constable tries to play the role of a petty king, that even the mail service is badly organized and the employees too lazy. In short, nothing works well, everybody complains. "It can last no longer, it will come to a bad end," they cry everywhere.

But, between this pacific arguing and insurrection or revolt, there is a wide abyss, — that abyss which, for the greatest part of humanity, lies between reasoning and action, thought and will, — the urge to act. How has this abyss been bridged? How is it that men who only yesterday were complaining quietly of their lot as they smoked their pipes, and the next moment were humbly saluting the local guard and gendarme whom they had just been abusing, — how is it that these same men a few days later were capable of seizing their scythes and their iron-shod pikes and attacking in his castle the lord who only yesterday was so formidable? By what miracle were these men, whose wives justly called them cowards, transformed in a day into heroes, marching through bullets and cannon balls to the conquest of their rights? How was it that *words*, so often spoken and lost in the air like the empty chiming of bells, were changed into *actions*?

The answer is easy.

The Spirit of Revolt

Action, the continuous action, ceaselessly renewed, of minorities brings about this transformation. Courage, devotion, the spirit of sacrifice, are as contagious as cowardice, submission, and panic.

What forms will this action take? All forms, indeed, the most varied forms, dictated by circumstances, temperament, and the means at disposal. Sometimes tragic, sometimes humorous, but always daring; sometimes collective, sometimes purely individual, this policy of action will neglect none of the means at hand, no event of public life, in order to keep the spirit alive, to propagate and find expression for dissatisfaction, to excite hatred against exploiters, to ridicule the government and expose its weakness, and above all and always, by actual example, to awaken courage and fan the spirit of revolt.

When a revolutionary situation arises in a country, before the spirit of revolt is sufficiently awakened in the masses to express itself in violent demonstrations in the streets or by rebellions and uprisings, it is through *action* that minorities succeed in awakening that feeling of independence and that spirit of audacity without which no revolution can come to a head.

Men of courage, not satisfied with words, but ever searching for the means to transform them into action, — men of integrity for whom the act is one with the idea, for whom prison, exile, and death are preferable to a life contrary to their principles, — intrepid souls who know that it is necessary to *dare* in order to succeed, — these are the lonely sentinels who enter the battle long before the masses are sufficiently roused to raise openly the banner of insurrection and to march, arms in hand, to the conquest of their rights.

In the midst of discontent, talk, theoretical discussions, an individual or collective act of revolt supervenes, symbolizing the dominant aspirations. It is possible that at the beginning the masses will remain indifferent. It is possible that while admiring the courage of the individual or the group which takes the initiative, the masses will at first follow those who are prudent and cautious, who will immediately describe this act as "insanity" and say that "those madmen, those fanatics will endanger everything."

They have calculated so well, those prudent and cautious men, that their party, slowly pursuing its work would, in a hundred years, two hundred years, three hundred years perhaps, succeed in conquering the whole world, — and now the unexpected intrudes! The unexpected, of course, is whatever has not been expected by them, — those prudent and cautious ones! Whoever has a slight knowledge of history and a fairly clear head knows perfectly well from the beginning that theoretical propaganda for revolution will necessarily express itself in action long before the theoreticians have decided that the moment to act has come. Nevertheless, the cautious theoreticians are angry at these madmen, they excommunicate them, they anathematize them. But the madmen win sympathy, the mass of the people secretly applaud their courage, and they find imitators. In proportion as the pioneers go to fill the jails and the penal colonies, others continue their work; acts of illegal protest, of revolt, of vengeance, multiply.

Indifference from this point on is impossible. Those who at the beginning never so much as asked what the "madmen" wanted, are compelled to think about them, to discuss their ideas, to take sides for or against. By actions which compel general attention, the new idea seeps into people's minds and wins converts. One such act may, in a few days, make more propaganda than thousands of pamphlets.

Above all, it awakens the spirit of revolt: it breeds daring. The old order, supported by the police, the magistrates, the *gendarmes* and the soldiers, appeared unshakable, like the old fortress of the Bastille, which also appeared impregnable to the eyes of the un-armed people gathered beneath its high walls equipped with loaded cannon. But soon it became apparent that the established order has not the force one had supposed. One courageous act has sufficed to upset in a few days the entire governmental machinery, to make the colossus tremble; another revolt has stirred a whole province into turmoil, and the army, till now always so imposing, has retreated before a handful of peasants armed with sticks and stones. The people observe that the monster is not so terrible as they thought they begin dimly to perceive that a few energetic efforts will be sufficient to throw it down. Hope is born in their hearts, and let us remember that if exasperation often drives men to revolt, it is always hope, the hope of victory, which makes revolutions.

The government resists; it is savage in

its repressions. But, though formerly persecution killed the energy of the oppressed, now, in periods of excitement, it produces the opposite result. It provokes new acts of revolt, individual and collective, it drives the rebels to heroism; and in rapid succession these acts spread, become general, develop. The revolutionary party is strengthened by elements which up to this time were hostile or indifferent to it. The general disintegration penetrates into the government, the ruling classes, the privileged; some of them advocate resistance to the limit; others are in favor of concessions; others, again, go so far as to declare themselves ready to renounce their privileges for the moment, in order to appease the spirit of revolt, hoping to dominate again later on. The unity of the government and the privileged class is broken.

The ruling classes may also try to find safety in savage reaction. But it is now too late; the battle only becomes more bitter, more terrible, and the revolution which is looming will only be more bloody. On the other hand, the smallest concession of the governing classes, since it comes too late, since it has been snatched in struggle, only awakes the revolutionary spirit still more.

The common people, who formerly would have been satisfied with the smallest concession, observe now that the enemy is wavering; they foresee victory, they feel their courage growing, and the same men who were formerly crushed by misery and were content to sigh in secret, now lift their heads and march proudly to the conquest of a better future.

Finally the revolution breaks out, the more terrible as the preceding struggles were bitter.

The direction which the revolution will take depends, no doubt, upon the sum total of the various circumstances that determine the coming of the cataclysm.

But it can be predicted in advance, according to the vigor of revolutionary action displayed in the preparatory period by the different progressive parties.

One party may have developed more clearly the theories which it defines and the program which it desires to realize; it may have made propaganda actively, by speech and in print. But it may not have sufficiently expressed its aspirations in the open, on the street, by actions which *embody the thought it represents*; it has done little, or it has done nothing against those who are its principal enemies; it has not attacked the institutions which it wants to demolish; its strength has been in theory, not in action; it has contributed little to awaken the spirit of revolt, or it has neglected to direct that spirit against conditions which it particularly desires to attack at the time of the revolution. As a result, this party is less known; its aspirations have not been daily and continuously affirmed by actions, the glamor of which could reach even the remotest hut; they have not sufficiently penetrated into the consciousness of the people; they have not identified themselves with the crowd and the street; they have never found simple expression in a popular slogan.

The most active writers of such a party are known by their readers as thinkers of great merit, but they have neither the reputation nor the capacities of men of action; and on the day when the mobs pour through the streets they will prefer to follow the advice of those who have less precise theoretical ideas and not such great aspirations, but whom they know better because they have seen them act.

The party which has made most revolutionary propaganda and which has shown most spirit and daring will be listened to on the day when it is necessary to act, to march in front in order to realize the revolution. But that party which has not had the daring to affirm itself by revolutionary acts in the preparatory periods nor had a driving force strong enough to inspire men and groups to the sentiment of abnegation, to the irresistible desire to put their ideas into practice (if this desire had existed it would have expressed itself in action long before the mass of the people had joined the revolt), and which did not know how to make its flag popular and its aspirations tangible and comprehensive — that party will have only a small chance of realizing even the least part of its program. It will be pushed aside by the parties of action.

These things we learn from the history of the periods which precede great revolutions. The revolutionary bourgeoisie understood this perfectly — it neglected no means of agitation to awaken the spirit of revolt when it tried to demolish the monarchical order. The French peasant of the eighteenth century understood it instinctively when it was a question of abolishing feudal rights; and the International acted in accordance with the same principles when it tried to awaken the

The Spirit of Revolt

spirit of revolt among the workers of the cities and to direct it against the natural enemy of the wage earner — the monopolizer of the means of production and of raw materials.

ARE WE GOOD ENOUGH?

One of the commonest objections to Communism is that men are not good enough to live under a Communist state of things. They would not submit to a compulsory Communism, but they are not yet ripe for free, Anarchistic Communism. Centuries of individualistic education have rendered them too egotistic. Slavery, submission to the strong, and work under the whip of necessity have rendered them unfit for a society where everybody would be free and know no compulsion except what results from a freely taken engagement towards the others, and their disapproval if he would not fulfill the engagement. Therefore, we are told, some intermediate transition state of society is necessary as a step towards Communism.

Old words in a new shape; words said

[141]

and repeated since the first attempt at any reform, political or social, in any human society. Words which we heard before the abolition of slavery; words said twenty and forty centuries ago by those who like too much their own quietness for liking rapid changes, whom boldness of thought frightens, and who themselves have not suffered enough from the iniquities of the present society to feel the deep necessity of new issues!

Men are not good enough for Communism, but are they good enough for Capitalism? If all men were good-hearted, kind, and just, they would never exploit one another, although possessing the means of doing so. With such men the private ownership of capital would be no danger. The capitalist would hasten to share his profits with the workers, and the best remunerated workers with those suffering from occasional causes. If men were provident they would not produce velvet and articles of luxury while food is wanted in cottages: they would not build palaces as long as there are slums.

If men had a deeply developed feeling of equity they would not oppress other men. Politicians would not cheat their electors; Parliament would not be a chattering and

cheating box, and Charles Warren's policemen would refuse to bludgeon the Trafalgar
Square talkers and listeners. And if men were
gallant, self-respecting, and less egotistic,
even a bad capitalist would not be a danger;
the workers would have soon reduced him to
the role of a simple comrade-manager. Even
a king would not be dangerous, because the
people would merely consider him as a fellow
unable to do better work, and therefore entrusted with signing some stupid papers sent
out to the other cranks calling themselves
kings.

But men are not those free-minded, independent, provident, loving, and compas-
sionate fellows which we should like to see
them. And precisely, therefore, they must
not continue living under the present system
which permits them to oppress and exploit
one another. Take, for instance, those misery-stricken tailors who paraded last Sunday
in the streets, and suppose that one of them
has inherited a hundred pounds from an
American uncle. With these hundred pounds
he surely will not start a productive association for a dozen of like misery-stricken tailors, and try to improve their condition. He
will become a sweater. And, therefore, we

say that in a society where men are so bad as this American heir, it is very hard for him to have misery-stricken tailors around him. As soon as he can he will sweat them; while if these same tailors had a secured living from the Communist stores, none of them would sweat to enrich their ex-comrade, and the young sweater would himself not become the very bad beast he surely will become if he continues to be a sweater.

We are told we are too slavish, too snobbish, to be placed under free institutions; but we say that because we are indeed so slavish we ought not to remain any longer under the present institutions, which favor the development of slavishness. We see that Britons, French, and Americans display the most disgusting slavishness towards Gladstone, Boulanger, or Gould. And we conclude that in a humanity already endowed with such slavish instincts it is very bad to have the masses forcibly deprived of higher education, and compelled to live under the present inequality of wealth, education, and knowledge. Higher instruction and equality of conditions would be the only means for destroying the inherited slavish instincts, and we cannot understand how slavish instincts can be made an argument for maintaining, even for one day longer, inequality of conditions; for refusing equality of instruction to all members of the community.

Our space is limited, but submit to the same analysis any of the aspects of our social life, and you will see that the present capitalist, authoritarian system is absolutely inappropriate to a society of men so improvident, so rapacious, so egotistic, and so slavish as they are now. Therefore, when we hear men saying that the Anarchists imagine men much better than they really are, we merely wonder how intelligent people can repeat that nonsense. Do we not say continually that the only means of rendering men less rapacious and egotistic, less ambitious and less slavish at the same time, is to eliminate those conditions which favor the growth of egotism and rapacity, of slavishness and ambition? The only difference between us and those who make the above objection is this: We do not, like them, exaggerate the inferior instincts of the masses, and do not complacently shut our eyes to the same bad instincts in the upper classes. We maintain that both rulers and ruled are spoiled by authority; *both* exploiters and exploited are spoiled by exploitation; while our opponents seem to admit that there is a kind of salt of the earth – the rulers, the employers, the leaders – who, happily enough, prevent those bad men – the ruled, the exploited, the led – from becoming still worse than they are.

There is the difference, and a very important one. *We* admit the imperfections of human nature, but we make no exception for the rulers. *They* make it, although sometimes unconsciously, and because we make no such exception, they say that we are dreamers, "unpractical men."

And old quarrel, that quarrel between the "practical men" and the "unpractical," the so-called Utopists: a quarrel renewed at each proposed change, and always terminating by the total defeat of those who name themselves practical people.

Many of us must remember the quarrel when it raged in America before the abolition of slavery. When the full emancipation of the Negroes was advocated, the practical people used to say that if the Negroes were no more compelled to labor by the whips of their owners, they would not work at all, and soon would become a charge upon the community. Thick whips could be prohibited, they said, and the thickness of the whips might be progressively reduced by law to half-an-inch first and then to a mere trifle of a few tenths of an inch; but some kind of whip must be maintained. And when the abolitionists said – just as we say now – that the enjoyment of the produce of one's labor would be a much more powerful inducement to work than the thickest whip. "Nonsense, my friend," they were told – just as we are told now. "You don't know human nature! Years of slavery have rendered them improvident, lazy and slavish, and human nature cannot be changed in one day. You are imbued, of course, with the best intentions, but you are quite 'unpractical.'"

Well, for sometime the practical men had their own way in elaborating schemes for the gradual emancipation of Negroes. But, alas!, the schemes proved quite unpractical, and the Civil War – the bloodiest on record – broke out. But the war resulted in the abolition of slavery, without any transition period – and see, none of the terrible consequences foreseen by the practical people followed. The Negroes work, they are industrious and laborious, they are provident – nay, too provident, indeed – and the only regret that can be expressed is, that the scheme advocated by the left wing of the unpractical camp – full equality and land allotments – was not realized. It would have saved much trouble now.

About the same time a like quarrel raged in Russia, and its cause was this: there were in Russia 20 million serfs. For generations past they had been under the rule, or rather the birch-rod, of their owners. They were flogged for tilling their soil badly, flogged for want of cleanliness in their households, flogged for imperfect weaving of their cloth, flogged for not sooner marrying their boys and girls – flogged for everything. Slavishness, improvidence, were their reputed characteristics.

Now came the Utopists and asked nothing short of the following: Complete liberation of the serfs; immediate abolition of any obligation of the serf towards the lord. More than that: immediate abolition of the lord's jurisdiction and his abandonment of all the affairs upon which he formerly judged, to peasants' tribunals elected by the peasants and judging, not in accordance with law which they do not know, but with their unwritten customs. Such was the unpractical scheme of the unpractical camp. It was treated as a mere folly by practical people.

But happily enough there was by that

time in Russia a good deal of unpracticalness in the air, and it was maintained by the
unpracticalness of the peasants, who revolted with sticks against guns, and refused to
submit, notwithstanding the massacres, and
thus enforced the unpractical state of mind
to such a degree as to permit the unpractical
camp to force the Tsar to sign their scheme
– still mutilated to some extent. The most
practical people hastened to flee away from
Russia, that they might not have their throats
cut a few days after the promulgation of that
unpractical scheme.

But everything went on quite smoothly,
notwithstanding the many blunders still committed by practical people. These slaves who
were reputed improvident, selfish brutes, and
so on, displayed such good sense, such an organizing capacity as to surpass the expectations of even the most unpractical Utopists;
and in three years after the Emancipation
the general physiognomy of the villages had
completely changed. The slaves were becoming Men!

The Utopists won the battle. They
proved that *they* were the really practical
people, and that those who pretended to be
practical were imbeciles. And the only regret

expressed now by all who know the Russian peasantry is, that too many concessions were made to those practical imbeciles and narrow-minded egotists: that the advice of the left wing of the unpractical camp was not followed in full.

We cannot give more examples. But we earnestly invite those who like to reason for themselves to study the history of any of the great social changes which have occurred in humanity from the rise of the Communes to the Reform and to our modern times. They will see that history is nothing but a struggle between the rulers and the ruled, the oppressors and the oppressed, in which struggle the practical camp always sides with the rulers and the oppressors, while the unpractical camp sides with the oppressed; and they will see that the struggle always ends in a final defeat of the practical camp after much bloodshed and suffering, due to what they call their "practical good sense."

If by saying that we are unpractical our opponents mean that we foresee the march of events better than the practical shortsighted cowards, then they are right. But if they mean that they, the practical people, have a better foresight of events, then we send them to history and ask them to put themselves in accordance with its teachings before making that presumptuous assertion.

Other Fine Titles from Trident Press:

Blood-Soaked Buddha/Hard Earth Pascal
by Noah Cicero

"Far too many books about Buddhism get bogged down in scholarly doublespeak. Others are full of far-fetched fantasies. Noah's book isn't like that. It's a real book for real people.

Brad Warner, author of Hardcore Zen

it gets cold
by j.avery

it gets cold demands a body that is both the haunting and the house, a queerness that is both living and dying. What can be gained by inhabiting this liminal space? What can the inhabitation of dying bring to the living? What can be done when it gets cold?

Major Diamonds Nights & Knives
by Katie Foster

MDNK is a poetry project modeled after a deck of cards. While writing this poem, Katie Foster felt possessed by a spirit who died in childbirth. She tried to tell her story as best she could.

Cactus
by Nathaniel Kennon Perkins

In *Cactus*, correctional officer and ex-punk rocker Will Stephens works guarding prisoners who pick up trash on the side of the highway. One of them, a hardened inmate with a tattoo of the Black Flag logo right beneath his eye, seems oddly familiar, but Will can't quite place him.

Sixty Tattoos I Secretly Gave Myself at Work
by Tanner Ballengee

STISGMAW is the most beautiful, the most vulnerable of punk and adventure memoirs. Each vignette centers around a hand-poked tattoo that the author gave himself while on the clock.

www.ingramcontent.com/pod-product-compliance
Lightning Source LLC
Chambersburg PA
CBHW070934030426
42336CB00014BA/2671